ML

ACPL ITEM
P9-AGS-866
DISCARDED

DO NOT REMOVE
CARDS FROM POCKET

SHEILAH'S
Fearless
Fussless
Cookbook

SHEILAH'S
Fearless
Fussless
Cookbook

More Easy Ways to Elegant Cooking

By Sheilah Kaufman
author of SHEILAH'S EASY WAYS TO ELEGANT COOKING

DELACORTE PRESS/ELEANOR FRIEDE

Published by
Delacorte Press/Eleanor Friede
1 Dag Hammarskjold Plaza
New York, New York 10017

Manufactured in the United States of America

First printing

Library of Congress Cataloging in Publication Data

Kaufman, Sheilah.
  Sheilah's fearless fussless cookbook.

  Includes index.
  1. Cookery. I. Title. II. Title: Fearless fussless
cookbook.
TX715.K2026   641.5   81-15241
ISBN 0-440-08176-9   AACR2

*This book is for my dear friends and relatives who had
the courage to taste my new creations along
the way and the faith to see me through.*

LEON AND PATTI

MARSHA AND DON

JUDY AND SHELLY

EDI AND DAVE

MYRNA

and, of course,

BARRY, DEBRA, AND JEFFREY

Contents

Introduction

Since the publication of my first book, *Sheilah's Easy Ways to Elegant Cooking,* I have demonstrated my recipes in department stores and gourmet shops from Alaska to Florida, from Hawaii to Maine, Texas, Ohio, and lots of places in between. I have enjoyed every minute of it, particularly meeting new friends who have shared their favorite recipes with me—some of which I am passing on to you in this book. I have tasted many new foods and combinations of foods: The variations seem to be endless, and that's what makes it so rewarding to be able to share them in a new volume.

I know a lot of people have liked my book because they write and tell me so: "I made Fettucini Alfredo last night. My husband is erecting a small shrine in the kitchen to store your book," and "Your ideas are a refreshing change from my old standards, and, best of all, they save time and money," and "This is the first time in my life I have really enjoyed cooking. I have discovered a new world."

After months of persuasion, a dear friend of mine, who is definitely not a cook, finally agreed to try a cake recipe. I gave her the recipe for Pineapple Pound Cake in this book. She called long distance, ecstatic, to tell me that everyone loved it and praised her and the cake. I congratulated her and said, "Now you can try the Apple Cake." "Never," she replied. "It's Pineapple Pound for life!" I hope other readers are more adventurous, for it is true that all my recipes are easy to make and virtually failure-proof.

One of the most popular features of *Sheilah's Easy Ways to Elegant Cooking* was the liberal sprinkling of helpful hints on all manner of topics throughout the book. It seems I learn something in the kitchen every day, and this book is filled with more hints to make your shopping and cooking easier and better.

My philosophy of cooking has not changed, and the second

book brings more of the same kind of easy ways to delicious meals. I am still basically lazy, and I like to cook when I feel like it, make a lot, and then freeze it for future use. That way I have to clean up only once and can enjoy my company and my parties when I entertain. I truly believe that cooking is an act of love: A meal should be a pleasure to prepare and should bring pleasure to the cook and the guests when it is served. Everything in this book is designed to make that happen. Again, I am grateful to my family and friends for helping me test the recipes in this book and for contributing some of their own favorites. And a special thanks to my long-time collaborator, Ginnie Manuel, whose help in transferring my kitchen adventures to the printed page is ever invaluable. Happy eating to all!

SHEILAH KAUFMAN
Potomac, Maryland
July 1981

The Fearless Cook's Guide to Substitutions

How many times, in a panic, have you found yourself out of an ingredient in the middle of preparing a recipe? Of course, reading a recipe thoroughly before starting out is the best way to avoid potential disasters; but in case you slip up, consult this list of substitutions. It might also prove helpful if you're trying to economize; for example, if you only need 1 square of unsweetened chocolate for a recipe, it's nice to know that powdered cocoa can be substituted, thus saving you the expense of buying a half-pound box of the chocolate. Additionally, you can use this guide when trying to cater to someone's food preferences.

ARROWROOT—2 teaspoons equal 1 tablespoon of cornstarch.

BREAD CRUMBS—1/4 cup of dry bread crumbs equals 1 slice of bread; 1/2 cup of soft bread crumbs equals 1 slice of bread.

BUTTER—1 cup equals 7/8 cup of oil or 14 tablespoons of solid shortening plus 1/2 teaspoon of salt.

BUTTERMILK—1 cup equals 1 cup of yogurt.

CATSUP—1/2 cup equals 1/2 cup of tomato sauce plus 2 tablespoons of sugar, 1 tablespoon of vinegar, and 1/8 teaspoon of ground cloves.

CHOCOLATE—1 ounce of unsweetened chocolate equals 3 tablespoons of carob powder plus 2 tablespoons of water; 1 ounce of unsweetened chocolate also equals 3 tablespoons of unsweetened cocoa plus 1 tablespoon of butter or other kind of fat.

CHOCOLATE (*semisweet*)—1 ounce of unsweetened chocolate plus 4 teaspoons of sugar equal 1 1/2 ounces of semi-sweet chocolate.

COFFEE—½ cup of strong brewed coffee equals 1 teaspoon of instant coffee dissolved in ½ cup of hot water.

CORN SYRUP—2 cups of corn syrup equal 1 cup of granulated sugar, but never use corn syrup to replace more than half the amount of sugar called for in a baking recipe.

CRACKER CRUMBS—¾ cup equals 1 cup of bread crumbs.

CREAM—1 cup of light (table) cream equals ⅞ cup of milk plus 3 tablespoons of butter; 1 cup of heavy cream equals ¾ cup of milk plus ½ cup of butter (for cooking only; this product will not whip).

CREAM (*whipped*)—1 cup of whipped cream equals ⅔ cup of well-chilled evaporated milk, whipped; or 1 cup of nonfat dry milk powder whipped with 1 cup of ice water.

EGG YOLKS—For thickening, 2 egg yolks equal 1 whole egg.

FLOUR—For thickening sauces, 1 tablespoon of flour equals 1 tablespoon of quick-cooking tapioca or 1½ teaspoons of cornstarch, potato starch, or arrowroot.

FLOUR (*cake*)—1 cup equals ⅞ cup of sifted all purpose flour; OR 1⅛ cups of cake flour equal 1 cup of all purpose flour.

FLOUR (*self-rising*)—1 cup equals 1 cup of all-purpose flour plus 1¼ teaspoons of baking powder and ⅛ teaspoon of salt.

GARLIC—1 clove equals ½ teaspoon of garlic powder or 1 teaspoon of garlic salt. (If using garlic salt, reduce salt called for in recipe by ½ teaspoon.)

GINGER—1 tablespoon of fresh ginger equals 1 teaspoon of powdered ginger or 1 tablespoon of candied ginger with the sugar washed off.

HERBS—1 tablespoon of fresh herbs equals 1½ teaspoons of dried.

HONEY—1 cup equals 1¼ cups of sugar. For baking, also decrease liquid in recipe by ¼ cup. If there is no other liquid in the recipe, add ¼ cup of flour. Unless sour cream or sour milk are used, also add a pinch of baking soda.

HOT PEPPER SAUCE—A few drops equal a dash of cayenne or red pepper.

LEMON JUICE—1 teaspoon equals ½ teaspoon of vinegar.

MILK—1 cup of whole milk equals ½ cup of evaporated milk plus ½ cup of water.

MUSHROOMS—6 ounces of canned, drained mushrooms equal ½ pound of fresh.

MUSTARD—1 tablespoon of prepared mustard equals 1 teaspoon of dried.

ONION—1 small fresh chopped onion equals 1 tablespoon of instant minced onion or ¼ cup of frozen chopped onion.

RAISINS—½ cup of raisins equals ½ cup of pitted prunes or dates, plumped and chopped.

SOUR CREAM—1 cup equals 3 tablespoons of butter plus ⅞ cup of buttermilk or yogurt. For low-calorie dips, 1 cup of sour cream equals 1 cup of cottage cheese pureed with ¼ cup of yogurt or buttermilk. 6 ounces of cream cheese plus enough milk to measure 1 cup can also be substituted for 1 cup of sour cream.

SOUR MILK—Place 1 tablespoon of lemon juice or distilled white vinegar in a measuring cup; add milk to measure 1 cup. Stir, and let the mixture clabber for about 5 minutes. Sour milk can be substituted for buttermilk.

SOY SAUCE—¼ cup equals 3 tablespoons of Worcestershire sauce plus 1 tablespoon of water.

SUGAR—1 cup equals 1¾ cups of confectioners' sugar, but do not substitute in baking.

SUGAR (*brown*)—1 cup firmly packed brown sugar equals 1 cup of granulated sugar plus 2 tablespoons of molasses.

TOMATOES—1 cup of canned tomatoes equals 1⅓ cups of fresh tomatoes, simmered.

TOMATO JUICE—3 cups equal 1½ cups of tomato sauce plus 1½ cups of water; or one 6-ounce can of tomato paste plus 3 cans of water, a dash of salt, and a dash of sugar.

TOMATO PASTE—1 tablespoon equals 1 tablespoon of catsup.

TOMATO PUREE—1 cup equals ½ cup of tomato paste plus ½ cup of water.

TOMATO SAUCE—1 cup equals 1 can of tomato paste plus 1½ cans of water plus desired seasonings.

WINE—For marinades, ½ cup equals ¼ cup of vinegar plus 1 tablespoon of sugar and ¼ cup of water.

WORCESTERSHIRE SAUCE—1 teaspoon equals 1 tablespoon of soy sauce plus a dash of hot pepper sauce.

YOGURT—1 cup equals 1 cup of buttermilk.

Hints About Herbs & Spices

Just as you experiment with different foods, you should also experiment with various seasonings. There is no "right" herb or spice for any food. In case you're wondering, herbs are derived from leaves, whereas spices include seeds (fennel, peppercorns) and bark (cinnamon).

Most herbs lose their essence quickly; so when long periods of cooking time are called for, they should be added near the end to insure maximum flavor. But allow enough time for them to blend with the other ingredients.

Whole spices or seeds should, on the other hand, be added to any given recipe at the beginning so that the cooking liquid has time to extract the flavors.

Add herbs and spices to uncooked foods (marinades, salad dressings, fruit compotes, cold appetizers) several hours before serving, so that the flavors have a chance to develop and blend.

Long storage causes most herbs and spices to deteriorate, herbs being the most fragile. If possible, buy them in leaf form, and crush them between your finger and thumb just before using. Ground spices will keep slightly longer, and whole spices and seeds retain their flavors the longest. To preserve freshness, store herbs and spices in airtight containers in a cool, dry place away from your stove. To test for freshness, take a sniff test. The characteristic aroma should greet you when you open the jar and bring it to your nose. If you can't distinguish what spice or herb it is, toss it out.

Several seasonings (such as chili powder, salt, and onion powder) lose their zip when the dish they're added to is subsequently frozen. It's best to taste the dish upon reheating it, adding more seasoning if necessary. By contrast, other flavorings (including black pepper, cloves, garlic, pimiento, celery salt, and imitation vanilla) increase in strength when frozen; so be sure to use these lightly.

Here are three different herb blends that you can make up in airtight jars and have on hand to add zest to everyday recipes:

HERB BLEND FOR SALADS:
4 parts each: marjoram, basil, tarragon, parsley, chervil, chives, dried celery leaves
1 part each: thyme, summer savory, rosemary

HERB BLEND FOR SOUPS:
2 parts each: thyme, parsley, chervil, basil, marjoram, dried celery leaves
1 part each: sage, rosemary, dried ground lemon peel

HERB BLEND FOR VEGETABLES:
1 part each: marjoram, basil, chervil, parsley, chives
Pinch of savory or thyme

Getting the Most from Fresh Produce

For the best-tasting recipes, the freshest produce should be used; all fruits and vegetables will be at their best when in season. Modern agricultural methods and storage techniques make most produce available year round, but that doesn't mean it will be at its best. (Have you ever tasted a tomato bought in January or an apple that has spent the entire fall and winter in cold storage?)

Fruit that is ripe and in season will have its own characteristic aroma that should be readily apparent. Weigh the fruit in your hand; if it feels heavy in relation to its size, that's a good indication it will be ripe and juicy on the inside.

Small pieces of fruit or vegetables tend to have more nutrients than large ones because vitamins and minerals are concentrated near the surface, and small produce has more surface in relation to its total size.

To insure that you are buying produce at the peak of freshness, follow this guide:

JANUARY—cabbage, eggplant, parsnips, potatoes

FEBRUARY—grapefruit, oranges

MARCH—asparagus, bananas, broccoli, green peas, mushrooms, spinach

APRIL—artichokes, asparagus, lettuce, mushrooms, green peas

MAY—cherries, cucumbers, pineapple, strawberries, tomatoes

JUNE—apricots, cherries, green beans, lemons, lettuce, strawberries, watermelon

JULY—beets, berries, cantaloupes, corn, grapes, limes, peaches, tomatoes

AUGUST—beets, corn, cucumbers, eggplant, honeydew, onions, peaches, plums

SEPTEMBER—grapes, pears

OCTOBER—apples, cauliflower, papayas, pears, squash

NOVEMBER—avocados, cauliflower, cranberries, papayas, squash, sweet potatoes

DECEMBER—avocados, coconuts

CHAPTER 1

APPETIZERS & FIRST COURSES

Meat
Seafood
Cheese
Vegetables
Soups

egg-
plant

lobster

spinach

bay
leaves

Meat

TABIBIAN LIVER PÂTÉ

*An excellent pâté to add an elegant touch to your party from
Patricia Tabibian, a fabulous cooking teacher in Delaware.*

1½ pounds chicken livers
⅓ cup dry sherry (do not use cooking sherry)
½ cup whipping cream
½ cup butter or margarine, softened
1 small onion, chopped
1 teaspoon salt
Freshly ground pepper to taste
½ teaspoon freshly ground nutmeg

The day before serving, clean the livers by removing any
fat or thick membranes.

Place the livers in a medium saucepan, and add just enough
water to cover them; simmer for 12 to 15 minutes, or until the
pink color is gone. Drain off the water.

In a blender or food processor, combine the livers and sherry;
slowly add the cream.

Add the remaining ingredients, and blend or process until
completely smooth.

Pour the mixture into an oiled mold or a serving bowl, and
place it in the refrigerator to chill overnight. (The mixture
will be thin and runny but will thicken with chilling.)

For maximum flavor, allow the pâté to sit at room temperature before serving. If you have placed it in a mold, turn it
out onto a serving platter, and garnish with parsley or lettuce
leaves.

This pâté tastes best when served with sliced French bread

and small pickles (*cornichons*). It can also be served with plain crackers.

Serves 8 to 12.

Note: Pâté can also be frozen for future use.

HINT

Solid and liquid volumes are different. Don't substitute a melted fat when a solid fat is specified.

WATERMELON WRAP-UPS

While I was teaching cooking in a Boston department store, a customer gave me this favorite recipe of hers. Sounds funny, but tastes great!

---

1 jar (any size) pickled watermelon rind, drained
½ pound bacon (cut strips in half)

Preheat oven to Broil.

Wrap each piece of pickled watermelon rind in a half strip of bacon.

Secure with toothpicks.

Place the wrap-ups on a rack over a shallow baking pan, and broil far enough away from the heat so that the toothpicks cannot catch fire.

Broil for 5 minutes.

Drain well on paper towels, and serve hot.

Makes about 1½ dozen.

REUBEN BALLS

3 ounces cream cheese, softened
1 can (1 pound) sauerkraut, drained and chopped
1 can (12 ounces) corned beef, chopped
¼ cup dry bread crumbs
1 cup flour
1 cup milk
1 cup cracker crumbs
Oil for deep frying

In a medium bowl, combine the cream cheese, sauerkraut, corned beef, and the bread crumbs, mixing well.

Shape the mixture into small balls, about 1 inch in diameter.

Dip the balls first in the flour, then in the milk, and finally in the cracker crumbs.

Using a deep fat fryer or an electric skillet with a thermometer, heat about 2 inches of oil to 375°F.

Fry the balls in hot oil for 2 to 3 minutes, or until golden.

Remove the balls to paper towels to drain.

Serve immediately, or if not using right away, let them cool and freeze. Frozen balls may be reheated in a 400°F oven for 10 minutes.

Makes about 5 dozen.

Seafood

BAKED SCALLOPS WITH FRAGRANT SAUCE

A very elegant appetizer for a special sit-down dinner. A food processor is necessary to prepare the fragrant sauce properly, although you could also use a blender.

1 whole egg
2 egg yolks
4 garlic cloves, minced
1 bunch fresh parsley with stems removed, minced
1¾ to 2 cups vegetable oil
Juice of 1 orange
Juice of 1 lemon
Salt and freshly ground pepper to taste
1 tablespoon butter
2 pounds fresh sea scallops, sliced crosswise

Place the egg and egg yolks in a food processor fitted with a steel blade, and process them until the mixture is yellow and foamy.

Add the minced garlic and parsley, and blend well.

With the motor still running, slowly add the oil through the feed tube, processing until the mixture is very thick.

Add the juices, and process a few seconds longer; add the salt and pepper to taste. (The sauce may be made in advance and refrigerated.)

Preheat the oven to 350°F. Have 8 individual ramekins ready.

Heat the butter in a large skillet, and gently sauté the scallops for about 3 minutes, or just until they begin to turn white.

Spoon the scallops evenly into the 8 ramekins, and top each portion with 2 heaping tablespoons of the sauce.

Bake until the sauce is light brown and bubbly, about 10 minutes.

Serves 8.

SHRIMP PÂTÉ

If you use canned or frozen cooked shrimp, this recipe only takes a minute. If you start with raw shrimp, it's a little more time-consuming but still a quick and easy spread.

---

1 pound fresh, frozen, or canned shrimp, peeled and
    cooked
2 tablespoons lemon juice
1½ teaspoons Dijon mustard
½ teaspoon mace
½ teaspoon cayenne pepper
¼ cup dry sherry
½ cup butter or margarine, softened

Place the shrimp in a blender or food processor, and quickly blend or process just enough to chop shrimp coarsely. (If you use a blender, you'll have to do this one third at a time.)

Add remaining ingredients, and blend or process just until ingredients are well combined.

Place the mixture in a serving bowl, cover, and refrigerate.

Allow pâté to warm up to room temperature before serving.

Serve with crackers, sliced French bread, or miniature rye bread.

Serves 12.

SALMON PÂTÉ

When presented in an earthenware crock, this pâté is a lovely hostess gift.

---

2 cups (1 pound) unsalted butter
1 can (16 ounces) red salmon, well drained, with bone
   and skin removed
½ teaspoon mace
½ teaspoon chili powder
2 tablespoons chopped parsley
2 teaspoons chopped chives
1 tablespoon lemon juice
2 to 3 teaspoons Five Chinese Spices (see below)

In a large bowl, with electric mixer at medium speed, cream the butter until fluffy.

Gradually add the salmon, beating at low speed until smooth.

Add the lemon juice and spices, and continue beating until smooth.

Place the mixture in several earthenware crocks or in a large serving bowl, cover, and refrigerate several hours.

Allow pâté to warm to room temperature before serving. Serve with crackers, sliced French bread, or miniature rye bread.

Serves 20 or more.

HINT

Five Chinese Spices is the name given to an unusual spice mixture made with equal parts of ground cinnamon, cloves, star anise, fennel, and Szechuan pepper. It can also be composed of cinnamon, cloves, ginger, nutmeg, and star anise.

EGG ROLLS

---

2 pounds egg-roll wrappers
2 tablespoons oil
½ pound ground pork tenderloin
1 pound uncooked shrimp, peeled and diced
8 black mushrooms
2 tablespoons dry sherry, slightly heated
5 ribs of celery, chopped
15 water chestnuts, chopped
½ pound fresh bean sprouts
1 bunch scallions, chopped
1 teaspoon sesame oil
½ teaspoon ground ginger
1 tablespoon salt
½ teaspoon sugar
1 tablespoon dry sherry
1 teaspoon cornstarch
1 teaspoon MSG (optional)
Oil for deep frying

Decide if you want regular-size or tiny (cocktail-size) egg rolls.

For regular size, cut the wrappers in half diagonally so that you have 2 large triangles. For tiny egg rolls, cut the large triangles in half again, making 4 small triangles.

In a large skillet over medium heat, heat 1 tablespoon of the oil, and cook the pork and shrimp for about 5 minutes.

Meanwhile, soak the black mushrooms in the 2 tablespoons of warm sherry; drain off the sherry, and reserve. Chop the mushrooms.

Place the pork and shrimp in a colander to drain, and add the remaining tablespoon of oil to the skillet.

Add the celery to the skillet, and sauté for 2 minutes.

Add the water chestnuts, mushrooms, reserved mushroom liquid, and bean sprouts to the skillet, and cook for 2 minutes.

Add the scallions, and return the pork and shrimp to the skillet, along with the remaining ingredients. Stir well, and cook 2 more minutes; pour the mixture into a colander to drain.

When the mixture is cool enough to handle, fill and fold the egg-roll wrappers according to the diagram.

In the same skillet, or in a deep fat fryer, heat about 2 inches of oil until very hot (400°F).

Fry the egg rolls, turning once, until golden brown. Drain them on paper towels, and serve hot with Chinese mustard or duck sauce.

If not serving right away, let egg rolls cool, place them in plastic bags or plastic wrap, and freeze until needed.

To serve from the freezer, place the frozen egg rolls on a cookie sheet, and bake in a preheated 375°F oven until hot.

Makes about 4 dozen small or 3 dozen large egg rolls.

TO FOLD EGG ROLL:

Bring point *A* to middle over filling; then do the same for point *B*. Wet egg-roll wrapper around all edges, and roll side *D* toward point *C*.

Leftover wrappers cut into thin strips and deep fried make great noodles.

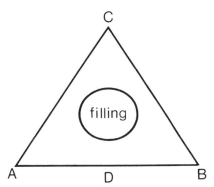

Cheese

APPLE CHUTNEY CHEESE BALLS

8 ounces cream cheese, softened
½ cup apple chutney
Dash of Tabasco sauce
1 cup chopped walnuts
½ cup finely chopped parsley
¼ cup Spanish paprika

In a medium bowl, using a wooden spoon, combine the cream cheese with the chutney and Tabasco until well blended.

Form the mixture into small balls, about 1 inch in diameter.

Roll one-third of the balls in the chopped walnuts, one-third of them in the parsley, and one-third in the paprika.

Arrange decoratively on a serving platter, and refrigerate until serving.

Makes about 2½ dozen.

TEXAS FUDGE

A favorite from my friends who wrote It's a Long Way to Guacamole! The Tex-Mex Cookbook. *This can be served hot or cold, and it can be frozen and reheated.*

---

1 pound Monterey Jack cheese, grated
1 pound cheddar cheese, grated
6 eggs, lightly beaten
1 can (5 ounces) evaporated milk
2 cans (4 ounces each) chopped green chilis, well drained

Preheat the oven to 350°F.

In a large bowl, combine the cheeses with the eggs and milk.

Line a 9 × 13-inch baking pan with the chilis, and cover with the cheese mixture.

Bake for 40 minutes.

Place the pan on a wire rack to cool slightly before cutting into bite-size squares. Serve hot or at room temperature.

Serves 12 to 15.

THREE CHEESE BOMBE

A most appealing appetizer to serve with French bread or crackers, but it also does double duty as a dessert after a hearty meal. Serve with a mixture of sliced apples and pears, grapes, orange sections, strawberries, and cracked walnuts.

2 envelopes unflavored gelatin
½ cup cold water
½ cup boiling water
⅔ cup grated Swiss cheese
⅔ cup crumbled bleu cheese
4 ounces Camembert cheese
4 egg yolks
2 cups whipping cream

The day before serving, butter a 1½-quart mold, and chill it until needed.

Sprinkle the gelatin over the cold water in a small bowl.

Add the boiling water, and stir until dissolved.

In a small bowl, with electric mixer at high speed, beat the three cheeses until smooth.

Add the egg yolks, beating well, and then add the dissolved gelatin.

Wash the beaters, and in a large bowl, with electric mixer at high speed, whip the cream until stiff; fold into the cheese mixture.

Let the mixture stand for 5 minutes before pouring it into the prepared mold. Refrigerate overnight.

Just before serving, unmold the cheese bombe by setting the mold in warm water for about 30 seconds and running a spatula or knife around the edges. Turn out onto a large serving platter, and garnish with fresh fruit if desired.

Serves 15 to 20.

MOCK BOURSIN

Boursin is a highly seasoned processed cheese that originated in France. This version is as good as the genuine article.

---

8 ounces cream cheese, softened
½ teaspoon garlic powder
1 tablespoon finely minced fresh parsley
½ teaspoon finely minced chives
½ teaspoon dried thyme leaves, crushed
Pinch of dried marjoram, finely crumbled
White pepper to taste

Using an electric mixer or a food processor, combine all the ingredients until the mixture is very smooth.

Place the cheese in a covered crock or bowl.

Refrigerate for at least 12 hours so that the flavor can develop.

To serve, spread on unflavored crackers or sliced French bread.

Serves 12.

CHEESE FINGERS

---

1 large loaf (22 ounces) white bread
1 pound cheddar cheese, sliced
½ pound processed bleu cheese
2 cups mayonnaise
2 cups grated Parmesan cheese

Preheat the oven to 350°F.

With a sharp knife, remove the crusts from the bread.

Place one slice of cheddar cheese on a slice of bread.

Place another slice of bread on top of that, and spread it with some of the bleu cheese.

On top of the bleu cheese, place a third slice of bread.

Spread all the sides with the mayonnaise, and dip all sides in the Parmesan.

Cut the sandwich into 4 "fingers" shaped like triangles or squares. Secure each section with a toothpick, and place the fingers on an ungreased cookie sheet.

Repeat the procedure with the remaining bread, cheeses, and mayonnaise.

Bake the fingers until the outside surfaces are brown, and the cheese has melted but not burned. Serve immediately.

Makes about 32 fingers.

SMOOTH AS SILK

1 pound cheddar cheese
3 hard-boiled eggs, peeled and quartered
1 pound sliced salami, cut into quarters
1 medium onion
¼ cup mayonnaise, or to taste
2 loaves miniature rye or pumpernickel bread
Paprika
1 teaspoon Worcestershire
Dash Tabasco

Preheat the oven to Broil.

Using a food processor fitted with the shredding disc, grate the cheddar cheese, and transfer it to a large bowl.

Refit the food processor with the steel blade, and finely chop the quartered eggs; add them to the cheese.

Chop the salami in the food processor, and add it to the cheese. Add Worcestershire and Tabasco.

Finally, cut the onion into chunks, and chop it finely in the food processor; add it to the cheese mixture.

Add the mayonnaise, mixing well. If necessary, add enough additional mayonnaise to bind the mixture nicely.

Place the bread slices on ungreased cookie sheets, and spread the mixture over each slice; sprinkle with paprika.

Broil, watching carefully, until the cheese melts—about 3 minutes.

Serves 12 to 15.

Vegetables

MUSHROOM DIP

6 ounces cream cheese, softened
1 tablespoon minced onion
1 cup finely chopped fresh mushrooms, uncooked
¼ teaspoon garlic salt
Freshly ground pepper to taste
1 tablespoon finely chopped parsley
1 teaspoon lemon juice

Using a food processor or electric mixer, whip the cream cheese with the onion until the mixture is light and fluffy.

Add the remaining ingredients, and mix well.

Refrigerate for at least 30 minutes.

Before serving, allow the mixture to return to room temperature. Serve with crackers or raw vegetables (including sliced fresh mushrooms).

Makes about 2 cups.

MUSHROOMS STUFFED WITH CLAMS

---

1 pound mushrooms
¼ cup melted butter
1 can (8 ounces) minced clams, drained
1 cup soft bread crumbs
2 eggs, slightly beaten
2 tablespoons chopped onion
6 tablespoons mayonnaise
2 teaspoons lemon juice
Freshly ground pepper to taste

Preheat the oven to 350°F.

Using a mushroom brush or a damp paper towel, clean the mushroom caps. Remove the stems, and set aside to use in soup or another recipe.

Using a pastry brush, brush the caps with the melted butter. Arrange the caps, open side up, in a shallow baking pan.

In a small bowl, combine the clams, bread crumbs, eggs, and onion with 4 tablespoons of the mayonnaise and 1 teaspoon of the lemon juice.

Fill each mushroom cap with a few teaspoons of this mixture.

Combine the remaining mayonnaise and lemon juice, and spoon a little on top of each mushroom.

Bake for 15 minutes, or until heated through.

Serves 12.

MUSHROOM ROLL–UPS

Another old favorite, which I dedicate to mushroom fanciers everywhere.

---

14 slices soft white bread
½ cup butter, softened
½ pound fresh mushrooms, finely chopped
2 tablespoons melted butter
½ teaspoon curry powder
1 tablespoon lemon juice
Salt and freshly ground pepper to taste
Pinch of cayenne pepper
½ cup melted butter

Preheat the oven to 425°F.

Remove the crusts from the bread, and roll each slice two or three times with a rolling pin until it is very thin.

Spread each slice of bread with the softened butter.

In a medium skillet, sauté the mushrooms in the 2 tablespoons of melted butter until the mushrooms are brown, and all liquid has evaporated.

Add the seasonings and the lemon juice, and mix well; remove from the heat.

Spread a tablespoon or more of the mushroom mixture on each slice of buttered bread.

Roll the bread up jelly-roll fashion, and brush the outside with the remaining melted butter.

Cut each roll into thirds, and arrange the slices on an ungreased cookie sheet.

Bake for 15 minutes, or until the roll-ups are lightly browned.

Makes about 3½ dozen.

MUSHROOM PUFFS

1 loaf white bread (16 to 22 ounces)
1 can (8 ounces) button mushrooms, well drained
8 ounces cream cheese and chives
2 egg yolks
2 tablespoons finely minced onion
$\frac{1}{2}$ teaspoon garlic powder
$\frac{1}{2}$ teaspoon seasoned salt
Freshly ground pepper to taste
Dash of Tabasco sauce

Preheat the oven to Broil.

Using a biscuit cutter, cut rounds about $1\frac{1}{2}$ to 2 inches in diameter from the slices of bread. Arrange them on an ungreased cookie sheet.

Place a button mushroom in the center of each bread circle.

In a small bowl, with a wooden spoon or electric mixer, combine the remaining ingredients, beating until the mixture is creamy.

Cover the mushrooms with the cheese mixture.

Place the cookie sheet in the oven, about 6 inches from the broiler, and bake until brown and puffy; watch them carefully, as it only takes a few seconds. Serve hot.

Makes about 3 dozen.

HINT

Save unused scraps of bread to make fresh bread crumbs, homemade stuffing, or bread pudding. If not using the bread right away, store in the freezer.

DOLMATHES

An exotic hors d'oeuvre of Greek origin.

---

1 jar (1 pound 9 ounces) grape leaves in brine
1 large onion, finely chopped
½ cup olive oil
1 cup raw long grain white rice
¼ cup minced parsley
2 tablespoons minced fresh dill or 1½ teaspoons dried
    dill weed
Salt and pepper to taste
¼ cup pine nuts
¼ cup currants
2½ cups beef or chicken stock
6 tablespoons lemon juice
1 cup water
Lemon wedges for garnish

Remove the grape leaves from the jar, and rinse them well under hot running water; drain the leaves well to squeeze out the liquid. Cut off the stems, and pat each leaf dry with paper towels.

In a large skillet, sauté the onion in ¼ cup of the olive oil until it is soft and golden.

Add the rice, parsley, dill, salt and pepper to taste, pine nuts, currants, and 1 cup of the stock; bring to a boil.

Lower the heat, and simmer, covered, until all liquid is absorbed—about 10 minutes. Let mixture cool slightly. Taste, and adjust seasonings.

To assemble Dolmathes, place a leaf, shiny side down, on a flat surface. Put approximately one teaspoon of the mixture in the center of the leaf. Fold over the sides like an envelope, and roll up the leaf. Be careful not to roll it too tightly, as the rice expands during the final cooking. Continue this procedure until all the leaves and filling are used up.

Line a deep, large heatproof pan with a few of the torn leaves or some lettuce leaves. (Or use cheesecloth to prevent the Dolmathes from sticking to the bottom of the pan.) Arrange the rolled up leaves in criss-crossing layers in the pan.

Sprinkle the leaves with the lemon juice and the remaining olive oil.

Pour the remaining stock and the water carefully down the sides of the pan. Weigh down the grape leaves with a large heatproof plate to prevent the rolls from opening up during the final cooking.

Cover the pan, and simmer for about 35 minutes, or until the rice is tender.

Let the rolls cool in the pan. Remove them to a serving platter with a slotted spoon, and refrigerate them until well chilled.

Just before serving, sprinkle some olive oil over the Dolmathes to make them shiny. Garnish with the lemon wedges.

Makes about 3 dozen.

Note: These do not freeze well, but they will keep in the refrigerator for several days.

SPINACH BALLS

2 packages (10 ounces each) frozen chopped spinach,
   cooked and drained
3 cups unseasoned package stuffing mix
1 large onion, finely chopped
6 eggs
¾ cup melted butter
½ cup grated Parmesan cheese
1 tablespoon garlic salt
½ teaspoon thyme
Freshly ground pepper to taste

In a large bowl, combine the spinach and stuffing mix, and add the chopped onion.

Beat the eggs well in a separate bowl, and add them to the spinach.

Add the remaining ingredients, blending well.

Roll the mixture into small balls, and place them on a cookie sheet or a tray in the freezer.

When frozen, wrap the spinach balls in foil, and store until needed.

About 1 hour before serving, remove the spinach balls from the freezer, and let them stand at room temperature (still wrapped in foil) while preheating the oven to 350°F.

Remove foil and bake the spinach balls for 30 minutes, or until thoroughly heated.

Makes about 3 dozen.

HINT

Spinach should be cooked in a stainless steel or enamel vessel, never aluminum, as the latter will give the spinach a metallic taste.

STUFFED ARTICHOKES

A distinctive hors d'oeuvre.

---

2 jars (11½ ounces each) artichoke hearts, well drained
5 hard-boiled eggs
1 tablespoon curry powder
2 tablespoons mayonnaise
2 tablespoons whipping cream
Salt and freshly ground pepper to taste

Blot the excess liquid from the artichoke hearts.

Press the yolks of the hard-boiled eggs through a sieve, discarding the whites.

Combine the yolks with the remaining ingredients to form a creamy mixture.

Place a medium-size "star" tip in a pastry bag, and fill the bag with the egg yolk mixture.

Pipe the egg yolk mixture through the pastry bag over each artichoke heart.

If not serving right away, refrigerate the artichoke hearts.

Makes about 2 dozen.

--- HINTS ---

For the best eating quality, eggs should be hard-boiled on low to moderate heat, as high temperatures and overcooking toughen them.

Use your oldest eggs for hard-boiled eggs, as fresh eggs when boiled tend to be very hard to peel.

ARTICHOKE DIP

Serve this unusual hot dip for a change of pace.

---

1 can (8½ ounces) artichoke hearts, drained
1 cup mayonnaise
1 cup grated Parmesan cheese
½ teaspoon garlic powder

Preheat the oven to 350°F.

Using a chef's knife or a food processor, coarsely chop the artichoke hearts.

Combine the artichoke hearts with the mayonnaise, cheese, and garlic powder, and spoon the mixture into a ramekin or other ovenproof dish.

Bake for 25 minutes.

Serve warm with breadsticks and/or fresh vegetables for dipping.

Serves 8 to 10.

HINT

Here's an imaginative way to serve chilled dips: Cut the top from one or more green peppers, and hollow them out. Use them as containers for your favorite dips.

CHILIES RELLENOS DIP

This is an all-time favorite recipe of a Norfolk, Virginia, family, who passed it on for me to share.

---

1 can (4 ounces) chopped chilies, well drained
1 can (6 ounces) pitted black olives, well drained
4 to 5 large ripe tomatoes, peeled
½ bunch scallions, chopped (including green tops)
½ cup red wine vinegar
¼ cup salad oil
Salt and freshly ground pepper to taste
Pinch of garlic powder, or to taste

The day before serving, place the chilies in a medium bowl; chop the olives, and combine them with the chilies.

Coarsely chop the tomatoes, and add them to the bowl, along with the scallions.

Mix in the vinegar, oil, and the seasonings, blending well.

Cover the bowl, and refrigerate overnight.

Before serving, taste and correct the seasonings. Serve with cheese chips, corn chips, crackers, or potato chips.

Makes about 3 cups.

CUCUMBER APPETIZER

---

1 large cucumber
3 ounces cream cheese, softened
1 tablespoon sour cream
1 tablespoon chopped chives
Salt and freshly ground pepper to taste

Peel the cucumber, and cut it in half lengthwise; scoop out the seeds, and discard them.

Combine the cream cheese, sour cream, chives, and salt and pepper to taste.

Spoon the cheese mixture into both the hollowed-out halves of the cucumber.

Chill the cucumber halves for at least 1 hour.

To serve, cut each half into thin slices, and serve them on miniature rye bread slices that have been lightly spread with mayonnaise.

Makes about 2 dozen.

HINT

Look for cucumbers with good green color that are firm over their entire length. They should not be too large in diameter. Good cucumbers may have many small lumps on their surfaces and some greenish-white color on their skins.

CUCUMBER SHREDS

2 medium cucumbers
1 clove garlic, crushed
5 tablespoons soy sauce
1 tablespoon sugar
5 tablespoons cider vinegar
¾ cup salad oil

Peel the cucumbers, cut them in half lengthwise, and scoop out the seeds.

Cut each of the halves into several small pieces, about 1 inch long × ½ inch wide.

In a medium bowl, combine the remaining ingredients, mixing well.

Add the cucumber pieces, tossing to coat well.

Cover the bowl, and refrigerate it for several hours to allow flavors to develop.

Just before serving, drain off the sauce, and spear the cucumber pieces with toothpicks.

Serves 6 to 8.

GUACAMOLE

A popular Mexican dip that goes best with Tortilla chips or corn chips.

---

4 very ripe avocados
2 to 3 tablespoons minced scallions
1 garlic clove, crushed
1 very ripe tomato, peeled and finely chopped
1½ teaspoons seasoned salt
⅛ teaspoon cayenne pepper
Pinch of ground cumin
Dash of lemon juice
2 to 3 tablespoons mayonnaise

Peel the avocados, and remove the seeds (set them aside for later); chop the avocados into small pieces.

Place the avocado pieces in a food processor or blender container; add the scallions, garlic, tomato, salt, cayenne, cumin, and lemon juice.

Blend or process the mixture until very smooth.

Add the mayonnaise, and blend or process until well combined.

Taste the guacamole, and adjust the seasonings to suit your taste.

Spoon the mixture into a serving bowl. If not serving immediately, place the avocado seeds on top, as they will keep the guacamole from discoloring. Refrigerate the mixture, and remove the seeds just before serving.

Serves 12 to 16.

Soups

AVOCADO VELVET SOUP

*A velvety smooth soup that can be served as a light summer
lunch or as the prelude to an elegant dinner.*

---

2 ripe avocados
1¾ cups canned or homemade chicken stock
1 cup sour cream
½ cup water
2 teaspoons lime juice
Salt and freshly ground pepper to taste
¼ teaspoon onion salt

Cut the avocados in half, peel them, and remove the seeds;
cut the avocados into small pieces.

Place the avocado pieces in a food processor or blender container, and process or blend until very smooth.

Add the chicken broth, sour cream, water, lime juice, and
the seasonings. Process or blend until very smooth.

Chill well until serving.

Serves 4.

HINTS

When making hot soups, if they taste too salty, slice up
a raw potato and drop it in. Remove and discard the
potato before serving.

To absorb excess fat from hot soups, place a lettuce leaf
in the kettle; remove and discard it before serving.

CUCUMBER SOUP

Quick and easy, this makes a lovely first course for a summer meal.

---

1 can (10¾ ounces) condensed cream of chicken soup
1 soup can of milk
3 scallions, finely chopped (including some of the green tops)
1 large cucumber

Place the chicken soup and milk in a food processor or blender container.

Add the scallions to the soup mixture.

Peel half of the cucumber, leaving the peel on the other half; cut both halves into quarters, and add them to the soup mixture.

Process or blend the mixture until very smooth.

Chill well until serving.

Serves 4.

CREAM OF MUSHROOM SOUP

A recipe from the "new cuisine," containing very little choles-terol.

---

1 cup skim milk ricotta cheese
1 cup skim or 2 percent milk
2 tablespoons vegetable oil
¾ pound fresh mushrooms, sliced
1 small onion, thinly sliced
2 cups canned or homemade chicken broth
Salt and freshly ground pepper to taste
Pinch of nutmeg

In a blender or food processor, combine the ricotta cheese with the milk, blending until smooth; set aside.

In a large kettle, heat the oil over medium heat. Add the mushrooms and onions, and cook, stirring frequently, for about 4 minutes.

Remove the kettle from the heat, and let the mushrooms cool thoroughly.

Add the ricotta-milk mixture, and stir for 1 or 2 minutes.

Then return the entire mixture to the blender or food processor, making sure it is thoroughly cool. Blend or process until smooth.

Return the mixture to the kettle, and add the chicken broth; cook gently over low heat just until the soup is heated. Do not allow to boil.

Add seasonings to taste, and serve the soup hot.

Serves 4 to 6.

HINT

There are all kinds of cooking oils—vegetable oil, corn oil, sunflower oil, etc. In most recipes, these can be used interchangeably, but both olive oil and peanut oil have a more distinctive flavor and should only be used when specifically called for.

AMBROSIA

One of my favorite cold soups, from Bon Appetit, an out-standing café in Philadelphia.

½ gallon orange juice
6 oranges, peeled (reserve peel)
1 cinnamon stick
½ of a fifth (about 1½ cups) of dark rum
½ cup dry sherry
½ to 1 cup superfine sugar
½ teaspoon ground cloves
2 cups shredded coconut
1 fresh pineapple, cubed
½ cup ground almonds
2 pints (4 cups) sour cream

Place the orange juice in a large heavy kettle, and cook over medium heat.

Grate the reserved orange peel, and add it to the juice.

Peel any remaining white skin or membrane from the oranges, and peel the orange sections, one half at a time, in a blender or food processor; add them to the kettle.

Add the cinnamon stick, rum, sherry, sugar, and cloves to the kettle, and bring to a boil.

Add the coconut, pineapple, and almonds; reduce the heat, and simmer for 15 minutes.

Stir in the sour cream, and chill the soup well before serving.

Serves 20.

EGGPLANT SOUP

½ cup corn oil
1 medium (about 2 pounds) eggplant, peeled and cubed
2 bunches scallions, chopped
3 garlic cloves, crushed
¼ cup flour
1 tablespoon curry powder
5 cups canned or homemade chicken broth
1 teaspoon rosemary
1 teaspoon marjoram
Freshly ground salt and pepper to taste
1¼ cups whipping cream

In a large skillet, heat the oil over medium-high heat, and sauté the eggplant cubes until they are light brown.

Remove the eggplant cubes from the skillet, and set aside; in the same skillet, sauté the scallions and garlic, adding a little more oil if necessary.

Stir in the flour and the curry powder with a wire whisk, blending well.

Add the chicken stock and the seasonings; mix well.

Add the eggplant cubes, and cook over medium heat for one-half hour.

Stir in the cream and heat slightly; do not overheat, or the soup will curdle. Serve immediately. (This soup can also be frozen and reheated.)

Serves 4 to 6.

CHAPTER 2

MAIN DISHES

Beef
Veal
Pork & Lamb
Chicken
Fish & Seafood
Meatless

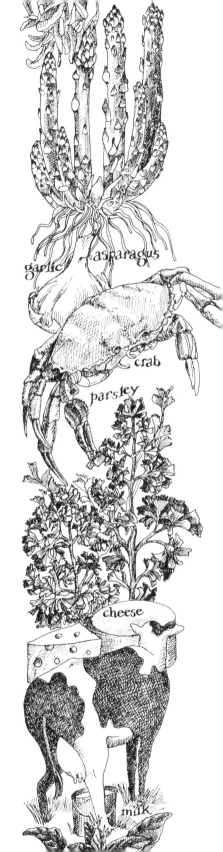

Beef

BEEF WELLINGTON

A real culinary challenge for that extra-special dinner party. You might want to try this on close friends or family before serving it at a formal dinner.

PASTRY:

> 4 cups flour
> 1 cup chilled unsalted butter, cut into small pieces
> 6 tablespoons vegetable shortening, chilled
> Pinch of salt
> 10 to 12 tablespoons ice water

LIVER PÂTÉ:

> 1 pound chicken livers
> 2 to 3 tablespoons butter or margarine
> 2 medium onions, finely chopped
> 2 tablespoons dry or medium sherry
> Pinch of thyme
> Pinch of rosemary
> 6 tablespoons softened butter
> Salt and pepper to taste
> 2 tablespoons sherry, optional
> 2 tablespoons brandy, optional

4-pound filet of beef (preferably butt tenderloin)
1 cup softened butter
Pinch of salt
Freshly ground pepper to taste
½ cup sliced celery
1 small onion, sliced
1 cup sliced carrots
⅓ cup chopped parsley
1 bay leaf
½ teaspoon rosemary
1 egg yolk, lightly beaten with 1 teaspoon of water

Several hours before serving, prepare the pastry: In a large chilled bowl, combine the flour, butter, shortening, and the salt.

Quickly, using your fingertips, blend the ingredients together until they resemble bits of coarse cornmeal.

All at once, pour 10 tablespoons of water over the mixture, and toss the mixture together lightly with a fork.

Gather the mixture into a ball; flatten it quickly with the heel of your hand, and gather the mixture back into a ball.

If the dough is crumbly, add the additional water, drop by drop.

Divide the dough in half, sprinkle each half with a little flour, and wrap each half in waxed paper.

Refrigerate the dough until firm, about 2 to 3 hours.

Meanwhile, prepare the pâté: In a large skillet, sauté the livers in the 2 to 3 tablespoons of butter for about 5 minutes, or until the livers are browned.

Add the onions, 2 tablespoons of the sherry, the thyme, and the rosemary; cook, stirring, until the onions are soft but not brown.

Using a blender or a food processor, puree the mixture about one-third at a time until it is smooth.

Turn the mixture into a bowl, and with a wooden spoon, beat in the softened butter, salt, and pepper.

Add the optional sherry and brandy if desired. Let the mixture cool completely before using it in the recipe. (This mixture also makes a nice spread for crackers or French bread as an appetizer.)

Preheat the oven to 475°F.

Spread the beef filet generously with the softened butter, and sprinkle it with the salt and pepper.

Place the celery, onion, carrot, parsley, bay leaf, and rosemary in the bottom of a shallow baking pan, and place the filet on top.

Roast the meat, uncovered, for 15 to 20 minutes.

Remove the meat from the oven; discard the vegetables, and let the meat cool completely.

About one-half hour before serving, spread the cooled roast with the liver pâté, covering it thoroughly.

Preheat the oven to 450°F.

Roll each half of the chilled pastry out on a floured surface to ⅛-inch thickness.

Place the filet on one half of the pastry; cover the top and sides of the meat with the other half of the pastry.

Trim the edges, moisten them with water, and press them together to seal the roast inside.

You may decorate the top of the pastry with leaves and flowers made out of any excess pastry.

Place the beef in a shallow baking pan, and brush the pastry with the egg yolk-water mixture. Prick the crust in a few places.

Bake the filet for 15 to 20 minutes for rare; do not over-bake.

To serve, cut into ½-inch slices against the grain.

Serves 6 to 8.

BEEF FILETS WITH BANANAS AND BAMBE SAUCE

3 pounds beef tenderloin
2 tablespoons oil
3 firm bananas
2 teaspoons butter
Salt, freshly ground pepper, and paprika to taste

BAMBE SAUCE:

3 tablespoons mango chutney
1 teaspoon curry powder
¼ cup butter
½ teaspoon powdered ginger
1 tablespoon lemon juice

Preheat the oven to Broil.

Rub the beef with the oil, and place it on a broiler pan. Broil 7 minutes on each side (for medium-rare), about 4 inches from the heat.

Meanwhile, cut the bananas in half lengthwise, and dot them with the butter.

During the last 5 minutes of cooking time, broil the bananas along with the meat.

As soon as the beef and bananas are done, remove them from the oven, and season the beef to taste. Keep the beef warm.

For the sauce, combine all the sauce ingredients in a medium saucepan and cook over medium heat until heated through.

To serve, slice the beef, and place it on a serving platter with the bananas; spoon the sauce on top.

Serves 6.

BOEUF MOUTARDE

4 to 5 pounds tenderloin filet, tied and at room
   temperature
3 tablespoons butter, softened
½ cup dry white wine
½ cup canned or homemade beef broth
¼ cup butter
¼ cup flour
¼ cup Dijon mustard
Salt and freshly ground pepper to taste
1 cup whipping cream

Preheat the oven to 500°F.

Rub the beef with the 3 tablespoons of softened butter, and place the filet in a roasting pan.

Roast the beef for 15 minutes, basting 2 or 3 times.

Skim the fat from the bottom of the pan, and continue roasting the beef for another 5 minutes.

Check the internal temperature with a meat thermometer, which should register 120°F for rare. Allow more time if necessary.

When the beef has reached the desired temperature, remove it from the oven, cover it with foil, and place it on a serving platter.

Skim the excess fat from the roasting pan drippings, and stir in the wine and the beef broth; set aside.

In a medium saucepan, melt the ¼ cup of butter over low heat, and stir in the flour; do not allow the roux to change color. Continue to stir the roux with a wire whisk for 2 more minutes.

Remove the saucepan from the heat, and add the wine mixture from the roasting pan.

Return the saucepan to the heat, and stir in the mustard and seasonings to taste.

Bring the sauce to a boil; reduce the heat, and simmer the sauce, gradually adding the whipping cream.

Correct the seasonings, adding more mustard if desired.

To serve, slice the beef, and spoon some of the sauce on top. Pass the remaining sauce separately.

Serves 8.

STOKES BARBECUE

---

3 to 4 pounds boneless beef chuck roast, trimmed of fat
2 onions, finely chopped
1 stalk celery, finely chopped
Salt and freshly ground pepper to taste

BARBECUE SAUCE:

½ cup butter or margarine, softened
2 tablespoons cider vinegar
1 tablespoon chili powder
1 teaspoon ground cumin
2 cups catsup
1 teaspoon garlic powder
2 tablespoons salad oil
1 teaspoon dry mustard or 2 teaspoons prepared mustard
Pinch of salt
⅛ teaspoon cayenne pepper
1 tablespoon lemon juice

Place the beef in a large kettle, along with the onion, celery, and salt and pepper to taste; add enough water to cover the meat.

Cover the kettle, and cook the beef over medium-low heat until the meat falls apart—about 3 hours.

Drain off the water, and keep the meat warm.

To make the barbecue sauce, combine all the ingredients

in a blender container or a food processor; blend or process until smooth.

Transfer the mixture to a medium saucepan, and cook over low heat, stirring occasionally, until heated through.

Add the sauce to the meat, mixing well.

Serve with hard rolls or sourdough bread.

Serves 6 to 8.

HINT

To revive limp celery, recrisp it in a pan of ice water to which you have added a slice of raw potato.

BEEF AND EGGPLANT PROVENÇALE

This dish has many of the virtues of Boeuf Bourguignon, which in fact it resembles. It can be made in advance, is relatively inexpensive for a large gathering, and most important, it is a robust, flavorful one-pot dish.

BEEF IN WINE:

⅓ cup salad oil
4½ pounds stew beef, cut into 1-inch cubes
1½ pounds small white onions
2 tablespoons flour
1 teaspoon sugar
1 tablespoon salt
½ teaspoon basil
½ teaspoon thyme
Freshly ground pepper to taste
Pinch of ground cloves
1 can (28 ounces) whole tomatoes, undrained
1½ cups dry red wine
2 bay leaves

EGGPLANT:

2 medium (about 2 pounds each) eggplants
3 eggs
1 cup fresh bread crumbs
¾ cup salad oil

GARNISH:

3 medium tomatoes
Salt
½ teaspoon thyme
2 tablespoons chopped parsley

Several hours or the day before serving, prepare the beef in wine: In a large heavy kettle, heat about 2 tablespoons of the oil.

Add the beef cubes, one third at a time, and cook over high heat until well browned on all sides. Remove the beef as it browns, and add more oil to the kettle as needed. Set the beef aside.

Meanwhile, in another saucepan, bring 2 quarts of water to a boil, and place the onions in the boiling water for 3 minutes.

Drain off the water, and let the onions cool. When they are cool enough to handle, peel them, and pare away the stem ends.

Using the same kettle in which the beef was browned, sauté the onions in the pan drippings until nicely browned on all sides. Remove the onions, and set them aside.

Remove the kettle from the heat, and stir in the flour, sugar, salt, basil, thyme, pepper to taste, and the cloves; stir to blend well.

Gradually add the tomatoes, the wine, bay leaves, and the browned beef cubes. Return the kettle to the heat, and bring the mixture to a boil.

Reduce the heat, cover the kettle, and simmer for about 2½ hours, stirring occasionally.

Add the browned onions to the kettle, and cook for another 40 minutes, or until the beef and onions are tender.

Remove the bay leaves, and discard them. Allow the beef mixture to cool to room temperature; then refrigerate it.

A few hours before serving, remove the mixture from the refrigerator, and let it stand while preparing the eggplant.

Wash each eggplant, and cut each one into ½-inch slices.

In a shallow dish, beat the eggs with ¼ cup water. Dip the eggplant slices first into the egg mixture, and then into the bread crumbs, coating them well.

In a large skillet, heat 2 tablespoons of the oil. Add the eggplant, a few slices at a time, and sauté them until golden brown on both sides.

Remove the eggplant, add more oil if necessary, and continue cooking the eggplant in the same manner.

Arrange the eggplant slices around the sides of a large (4-quart) shallow casserole, and lay some of the slices over the bottom. It will be necessary to overlap the slices. Cover the casserole, and set it aside.

Prepare the garnish by cutting each tomato into 6 wedges. Sprinkle them with the salt and thyme, and let them stand at room temperature.

About ½ hour before serving, preheat the oven to 350°F.

Bake the eggplant, covered, for 25 minutes, or until piping hot. Do not overcook the eggplant, or it will become soggy.

At the same time, reheat the beef in wine on top of the stove until the mixture boils; reduce the heat, and simmer until the beef is well heated.

Spoon the beef into the eggplant-lined casserole. Arrange the tomato wedges, overlapping, around the edge of the casserole, and sprinkle with the chopped parsley.

Serve with French bread and boiled potatoes.

Serves 10 to 12.

HINT

A level teaspoon of sugar added to a can of tomatoes cuts the acidic taste.

BEST BRISKET EVER

This recipe yields a marvelous sauce that is delicious with rice or noodles.

---

3 pounds beef brisket
1 envelope dry onion soup mix
1 can (16 ounces) jellied cranberry sauce
Freshly ground pepper to taste
½ cup water

Preheat the oven to 325°F.

Place the brisket in a large roasting pan.

Pour the dried soup over the meat.

Spread the jellied cranberry sauce on top of the soup mix.

Season the roast with pepper to taste, and pour the water into the pan around the sides of the beef.

Cover the pan, and bake for 3 hours, or until the meat is very tender, stirring the sauce once during baking time to mix all the ingredients.

Remove the brisket from the pan, and place it on a serving platter; cut into thick slices.

Skim the fat from the top of the sauce; pour some over the brisket, and pass the rest separately.

Serves 6.

CHICKEN FRIED STEAK

I discovered this Texas favorite while cooking at Joske's in Houston.

1½ pounds round steak, tenderized*
1 cup flour
Salt and freshly ground pepper to taste
2 teaspoons chili powder, or more to taste
1 cup buttermilk
1 cup corn oil for frying

Cut the steak into 4 or 5 serving pieces.

In a shallow bowl, combine the flour, salt, pepper, and chili powder.

Place the buttermilk in another bowl, and dip the steak pieces first into the buttermilk and then into the flour mixture.

If a heavy crust is desired, dip the pieces into the buttermilk and flour a second time.

Heat about 1 inch of oil in a skillet or electric fry pan over high heat; add the steak, and cook the pieces until they are brown on both sides, turning once.

Drain the meat on paper towels; if not serving immediately, keep warm. Serve with Cream Gravy. (See page 59.)

* Use a commercial tenderizer, following label directions.

CREAM GRAVY

3 tablespoons oil from pan
3 tablespoons flour (using any left over from dredging
  meat)
1 to 1½ cups buttermilk (use what was left over from
  dipping bowl, above)

Pour off from the steak skillet all except 3 tablespoons of cooking oil and whatever has stuck to the bottom of the pan.

Stir in the flour, continuing to stir until smooth. Heat very slowly. When the flour begins to brown slightly, gradually pour in milk and stir constantly until thick. Let gravy boil lightly for 4 to 5 minutes. Taste for seasoning and correct if necessary.

Serves 4.

MEATBALLS IN SOUR CREAM & DILL SAUCE

Besides making an interesting main course, these can also be served as an appetizer.

---

2 tablespoons unseasoned bread crumbs
¼ cup table cream
1 pound ground chuck or round
½ pound ground veal
¼ cup finely diced beef marrow or 3 tablespoons softened
    butter
5 tablespoons butter or margarine
1 medium onion, finely chopped
1½ tablespoons finely chopped shallots
½ teaspoon garlic powder
1 teaspoon grated lemon peel
2 tablespoons finely chopped parsley
Salt and freshly ground pepper to taste
½ teaspoon thyme
2 eggs
2 tablespoons vegetable oil

SAUCE:

3 tablespoons butter or margarine
2 tablespoons flour
1 cup canned or homemade beef broth
½ cup sour cream
1 tablespoon dill weed
¼ teaspoon lemon juice
Pinch of cayenne pepper
Salt to taste

Prepare meatballs at least 2 hours before serving, so they can chill before being cooked.

In a large bowl, soak the bread crumbs in the cream for 5 minutes.

Add the ground beef, ground veal, and the marrow or softened butter.

In a small skillet, melt 2 tablespoons of the butter, and sauté the onion and shallots for 3 minutes. Add this to the meat mixture, along with the garlic powder, lemon peel, parsley, salt and pepper to taste, and the thyme.

Beat the eggs lightly, and pour them over the meat mixture, tossing until well combined.

Form the mixture into small meatballs, about 1 inch in diameter. Place them on a cookie sheet lined with waxed paper, and refrigerate for 1 hour.

To cook the meatballs, heat the remaining 3 tablespoons of butter with the oil in a large skillet over medium-high heat.

When the butter-oil mixture is hot, add enough meatballs to cover the bottom of the pan. Brown the meatballs by sliding the skillet back and forth. (This helps browning to take place evenly.)

After a few minutes, reduce the heat, and cook for about 6 more minutes, or until the meatballs are well done.

Transfer the meatballs, using a slotted spoon, to a large, shallow casserole. If necessary, repeat the process with any remaining meatballs. Keep the meatballs warm while preparing the sauce.

Use the same skillet to prepare the sauce: melt the butter over low heat.

Remove the skillet from the heat, and stir in the flour with a wire whisk, stirring well for 2 minutes.

Add the beef stock, and return the skillet to the heat. Increase the heat to medium, and continue to stir the sauce until it begins to boil and thicken.

Reduce the heat to low, and stir in the sour cream a spoonful at a time.

Add the dill, lemon juice, cayenne, and salt to taste.

Stir for another minute, and pour the sauce over the meatballs. Serve hot with boiled white rice or noodles.

Serves 4.

EMPANADAS

These Mexican-style meat pies can be served as a main dish or an appetizer.

PASTRY:

1 cup softened butter or margarine
2 packages (3 ounces each) cream cheese, softened
2 cups sifted flour

PICADILLO FILLING:

1 pound ground beef
1½ tablespoons olive oil
1 small onion, chopped
1 garlic clove, minced
2 tomatoes, peeled, seeded, and coarsely chopped
1 apple, peeled, cored, and coarsely chopped
2 canned jalapeño chilis, drained, rinsed, and seeded
⅓ cup raisins
5 pimiento-stuffed green olives, cut in half
¼ teaspoon cinnamon
¼ teaspoon ground cumin
Pinch of ground cloves
¼ cup blanched, slivered almonds

TOPPING:

1 egg
1 tablespoon water

The day before serving, prepare the pastry: in a large bowl, with the electric mixer at medium speed, cream the butter and cream cheese until fluffy.

With a wooden spoon, blend in the flour, mixing to form a smooth dough.

Form the dough into a ball, wrap in foil or plastic wrap, and refrigerate it overnight.

About 1½ hours before serving, prepare the Picadillo filling: brown the beef in 1 tablespoon of the olive oil in a large skillet over high heat; break up any lumps of meat.

When the meat has lost all its pink color, add the onions and garlic, stirring well; cook over medium heat for about 4 minutes.

Add the tomatoes and the apples.

Slice the jalapeños crosswise into ⅛-inch slices, and add them to the skillet, along with the raisins, olives, cinnamon, cumin, and cloves.

Simmer the mixture, uncovered, over low heat for 20 minutes.

Meanwhile, in a small saucepan or skillet, heat the remaining ½ tablespoon of olive oil, making sure the bottom is well coated. Add the almonds, and fry them for about 2 minutes, or until they are golden brown. Be careful not to burn them. Drain the almonds on a paper towel.

Add the almonds to the Picadillo, and remove the skillet from the heat; let the mixture cool to room temperature.

Preheat the oven to 400°F.

Remove the dough from the refrigerator, and working with one half at a time, roll it out on a lightly floured surface to ⅛-inch thickness.

Using a 2-inch-round biscuit or cookie cutter (or an empty juice can), cut out rounds. Keep gathering up scraps of dough, rerolling them and cutting out more rounds.

Place about 1½ teaspoons of the filling on each round of dough, and fold it in half; crimp the edges to seal the filling. Repeat with the remaining dough and filling.

Beat the empanadas on one or more lightly greased cookie sheets; combine the egg with the water, and brush the mixture on the top and around the edges of each empanada.

Bake for 12 to 15 minutes, or until the empanadas are golden brown.

Makes 3 to 3½ dozen; serves 6 to 8.

Note: Filled empanadas can also be frozen and baked directly from the freezer in a 400°F oven for 15 to 20 minutes.

COLORADO CASSEROLE

A hearty one-pot main dish that enables you to stretch a small amount of ground beef without skimping on flavor or nutrition.

MEATBALLS:

1 pound ground beef
⅛ teaspoon garlic powder
1 tablespoon instant minced onion (or 1 small onion, finely chopped)
½ teaspoon chili powder
1 egg
½ teaspoon salt
¾ cup unseasoned bread crumbs

1½ cups long grain raw white rice
1 can (15 ounces) chick-peas, drained
1 can (16 ounces) red kidney beans, drained
¼ teaspoon garlic powder
1 cup cottage cheese
1 can (4 ounces) chopped green chilis, drained
2 drops Tabasco sauce
1½ cups grated cheddar cheese

Preheat the oven to 350°F.

To make the meatballs, mix the ground beef with the ⅛ teaspoon of garlic powder, the onion, chili powder, egg, salt, and bread crumbs.

Form the mixture into about 60 little meatballs, and place them on a large baking sheet; bake for 15 minutes, or until brown.

Remove the pan from the oven, drain off the fat, and set aside.

Meanwhile, cook the rice according to the package directions.

In a 3-quart casserole, combine the cooked rice with the

chick-peas, kidney beans, garlic powder, cottage cheese, chilis, Tabasco sauce, and 1 cup of the grated cheddar.

Carefully stir in the meatballs, and sprinkle the remaining cheese on top.

Bake the casserole, covered, for 30 minutes, or until heated through.

Serves 6 to 8.

STUFFED ZUCCHINI

---

6 medium zucchini
3 tablespoons butter or margarine
1 medium onion, finely chopped
½ pound ground beef
Salt and freshly ground pepper to taste
1 teaspoon dill weed
2 cans (8 ounces each) tomato sauce
1½ cups long grain raw white rice

Cut the zucchini in half lengthwise, and hollow them out.

Melt the butter in a large skillet, and sauté the onion over medium heat.

Add the ground beef, and cook until it browns.

Add salt and pepper to taste, the dill, and 1 can of the tomato sauce; bring to a boil, and add the rice.

Immediately remove the skillet from the heat, and use the mixture to stuff the hollowed-out zucchini.

Set the stuffed zucchini in a large, deep kettle or skillet.

Combine the remaining can of tomato sauce with 1 can of water, and pour this mixture over the zucchini and into the bottom of the kettle.

Cover the kettle, and bring to a boil; reduce the heat, and simmer until the rice is cooked, about 40 minutes.

Serves 4 to 6.

ZUCCHINI LASAGNE

The surprise here is that zucchini replaces the customary pasta,
thus saving calories but not skimping on flavor.

---

1 pound ground beef
1 can (12 ounces) tomato paste
½ teaspoon oregano
½ teaspoon basil
Salt and freshly ground pepper to taste
3 large zucchini
2 cups creamed cottage cheese
2 eggs
1 tablespoon flour
½ to ¾ cup grated mozzarella cheese

Preheat the oven to 375°F.

In a large skillet, brown the beef, and drain off the excess fat.

Add the tomato paste and the seasonings, and simmer for about 5 minutes, stirring occasionally.

Cut the zucchini into ⅛-inch slices.

In a medium bowl, combine the cottage cheese with the eggs, mixing well.

Place one-half of the zucchini slices in a large, shallow baking dish, and sprinkle them with the flour.

Cover the zucchini with one-half of the cottage cheese mixture, and top that with half of the meat mixture.

Place the remaining zucchini slices over the meat mixture, then the remaining cottage cheese, and finally the remaining meat sauce.

Sprinkle the mozzarella over the top, and bake the lasagne for 30 to 40 minutes, or until hot and bubbly.

Serves 6.

CANNELLONI

Most ground beef recipes lend themselves to informal enter-taining. This one, which also includes chicken livers, is elegant enough to serve at a special sit-down dinner.

CRÊPES:

1½ cups milk
3 eggs
1½ cups flour
1 teaspoon melted butter, plus more for cooking

FILLING:

2 tablespoons butter or margarine
1 pound chicken livers
1 large onion, finely chopped
1 garlic clove, crushed
½ pound ground beef
1 teaspoon salt
¼ teaspoon sage
¼ teaspoon thyme
¾ cup freshly grated Parmesan cheese (reserve ½ cup
    for topping)

SAUCE:

3 tablespoons butter or margarine
3 tablespoons flour
1½ cups milk
⅛ teaspoon nutmeg

Several hours before serving, prepare the crêpes.

Place the milk and eggs in a blender container or food processor; add the flour and butter, and blend or process at high speed to form a smooth batter. Let the batter stand at room temperature for about 1 hour to allow the flour to dis-solve thoroughly.

Heat a 7- or 8-inch crêpe pan over medium-high heat for about 3 minutes; remove the pan from the heat, and brush it with melted butter.

Using a ladle or a small measuring cup, pour about 2 tablespoons of batter into the pan, rotating the pan to insure that the batter covers the bottom (not the sides) quickly and evenly.

Cook until the crêpe is dry on the top, and using a flexible spatula, turn it over; cook about 15 seconds longer, or until lightly browned.

Slide the crêpe out of its pan onto a wire rack, and repeat the process. Stack the crêpes as you cook them. Brush the pan with melted butter about every other crêpe. You should have 16 to 18 crêpes. If not using them right away, keep them covered with a damp cloth.

To make the filling, melt 2 tablespoons of butter in a large skillet, and sauté the chicken livers until they are brown; remove them with a slotted spoon, and set them aside.

In the same skillet, sauté the onion and garlic until they are tender.

Add the beef, and continue cooking until it is brown; remove from the heat.

With a chef's knife or food processor, finely mince the chicken livers, and add them to the skillet, along with the seasonings and ¼ cup of the Parmesan.

Preheat the oven to 350°F.

To make the sauce, melt the butter in a small saucepan over low heat.

With a wire whisk, stir in the flour, beating until smooth.

Remove the pan from the heat, and gradually add the milk; return the saucepan to medium heat, and cook, stirring constantly, until the sauce has thickened. Stir in the nutmeg, and remove from the heat.

To assemble the cannelloni, place about 2 tablespoons of the filling in the center of each crêpe; roll it up and place it, seam side down, in a greased shallow baking pan. Repeat with the remaining crêpes and filling.

Spoon the sauce over the crêpes, and sprinkle with the remaining Parmesan. (The dish may be frozen at this point if desired.)

Bake, uncovered, for 20 minutes, or until the sauce is bubbly. If baking the cannelloni directly from the freezer, increase the baking time to 45 minutes.

Serves 6 to 8.

Veal

VEAL AFRICAN

Fork-tender and slightly piquant.

12 veal scallopini
Salt and freshly ground pepper to taste
6 firm bananas, peeled and sliced in half
½ cup flour
3 tablespoons vegetable oil

CURRY SAUCE:

1 medium onion, finely chopped
¼ teaspoon dry mustard
½ cup butter or margarine
1 apple, peeled and sliced
2 tablespoons flour
1¼ teaspoons curry powder
Freshly ground nutmeg to taste
2½ cups canned or homemade chicken broth
½ cup flaked coconut

Season the veal with the salt and pepper; roll each scallop around a banana half, and secure with a toothpick.

Dust the veal lightly with the flour.

Heat the oil in a large skillet, and sauté the veal until lightly brown on all sides.

Remove the toothpicks from the veal rolls, and keep the veal and banana intact; place them in a large shallow casserole.

Prepare the curry sauce: combine the onion with the dry mustard.

Melt the butter in a medium saucepan, and add the onion-mustard mixture and the apple slices; cook over low heat for about 5 minutes.

Add the flour, the curry powder, and the nutmeg, mixing well; cook for another 3 or 4 minutes.

Add the chicken broth, stirring well; simmer, covered, for 45 minutes.

Preheat the oven to 350°F.

Add the coconut to the sauce, and simmer for another 10 minutes.

Strain the sauce, and pour it over the veal.

Bake the veal, uncovered, for about 10 minutes, or until the sauce is bubbly.

Serve garnished with coconut, chopped egg, chopped parsley, and raisins.

Serves 6.

HINTS

When choosing between butter and margarine for cooking, remember that butter adds flavor to the dish; margarine is neutral and contributes little taste. When other ingredients in a given dish are very emphatic, the flavor of butter becomes less important.

Always cover butter when storing it in the refrigerator, so that it does not absorb the flavors of other foods.

A plain pan gravy that has been deglazed with broth or wine is enhanced by the addition of a tablespoon or two of butter swirled into the sauce just before serving. Remove the pan from the heat, and beat in the butter one half tablespoon at a time.

VEAL DUXELLES

Duxelles is a kind of mushroom hash, which gives this dish its distinctive flavor.

½ cup olive oil (approximately)
¼ cup butter
1 large onion, finely chopped
2 shallots, minced
1 pound mushrooms, finely chopped
1 tablespoon lemon juice
3 garlic cloves, minced
½ cup chopped parsley
2 to 3 tablespoons tomato paste
Salt and freshly ground pepper to taste
1 egg, lightly beaten
4 veal cutlets
3 tablespoons unsalted butter

Using either parchment paper or aluminum foil, cut out 8 pieces, 8 × 6 inches each; brush one side of each sheet with olive oil, using about 2 tablespoons in all.

Melt the ¼ cup of butter in a large skillet, and sauté the onion, shallots, and mushrooms for 3 minutes over medium-high heat.

Add the lemon juice, and cook another 5 minutes, or until the mixture is dry.

Add the garlic and parsley, and cook for another minute.

Add the tomato paste, and salt and pepper to taste; mix well.

Remove the skillet from the heat, and stir in the beaten egg; return the skillet to low heat, and cook, stirring, until the mixture is thickened. Remove the skillet from the heat, and let the duxelles cool.

Preheat the oven to 350°F.

Brush the veal cutlets with some of the olive oil.

In another skillet, heat the unsalted butter with the remaining olive oil, and sauté the veal cutlets until they are nicely browned. Remove from the heat.

Place a large spoonful of the duxelles on each of 4 pieces of the oiled paper or foil. Cover each spoonful with a veal cutlet, and spoon the remaining duxelles evenly over the cutlets.

Top with the remaining 4 pieces of paper or foil, oiled side down.

Fold the paper or foil to enclose the meat; then fold the edges twice, so that the filling cannot seep out.

Place the "packages" on a baking sheet, and bake them for 15 to 20 minutes.

Serve each piece of veal still wrapped in its paper.

Serves 4.

HINT

The milk solids in unclarified butter burn easily; so, when butter must be subjected to high heat, add oil to raise the burning point at a ratio of 1 tablespoon of oil to 2 tablespoons of butter.

OSSO BUCCO

This one-pot dish is grand for cold-weather dining. It can be prepared in advance and frozen.

⅓ cup flour
1 teaspoon salt
¼ teaspoon freshly ground pepper
3 to 4 veal shanks (with meat on the bone), cut into 3-inch pieces
3 tablespoons olive oil
1 large onion, coarsely chopped
1½ cups coarsely chopped carrots
1½ cups coarsely chopped celery
2 garlic cloves, crushed
2 tomatoes, peeled and coarsely chopped
1½ cups dry white wine
1 teaspoon basil
1 teaspoon thyme
1 bay leaf
3 tablespoons chopped parsley

Combine the flour with the salt and pepper, and dredge the veal shanks in this mixture; shake off the excess flour.

Heat the oil in a large kettle, and brown the veal on both sides; remove the veal as it browns, and set it aside.

In the same kettle, adding more oil if necessary, sauté the onion, carrots, celery, and garlic for 3 minutes.

Add the tomatoes, wine, basil, thyme, and the bay leaf, mixing well.

Bring the mixture to a boil; return the veal to the kettle, lower the heat, and simmer, covered, for about 2 hours. (If there does not appear to be enough liquid in the kettle, add more wine.)

Taste, and correct the seasonings. Just before serving, remove the bay leaf, and add the parsley.

Serve with rice or noodles.

Serves 4.

BLANQUETTE DE VEAU

A rather complicated dish, but your patience will be rewarded with an exquisite entrée.

2½ to 3 pounds, boneless breast or shoulder of veal,
    cubed
2 carrots, peeled and sliced
2 medium whole onions, each pierced with 2 cloves
1 leek, sliced
1 stalk of celery with the leaves
1 bouquet garni (1 bay leaf, 1 teaspoon thyme leaves,
    1 sprig of parsley wrapped in cheesecloth)
Salt and freshly ground pepper to taste
1 garlic clove, split
1 can (16 ounces) pearl onions, drained
¾ pound mushrooms, sliced
½ cup water
½ teaspoon salt
Juice of ½ lemon
7 tablespoons butter
3 tablespoons flour
2 egg yolks
½ cup sour cream

Place the veal in a large kettle, cover it with cold water, and bring it to a boil.

Boil the veal for 5 minutes, or until it turns white; drain, and rinse with fresh water.

Return the meat to the kettle with fresh water, and bring it to a boil again; add the carrots, onions, leek, celery, the bouquet garni, salt and pepper to taste, and the garlic.

Cover the kettle with waxed paper and a tight-fitting lid, and lower the heat; simmer the veal for 1 to 1½ hours, or until it is tender—do not overcook.

Remove the meat to a serving dish or casserole, reserving

the cooking liquid. Keep the meat warm while you complete the recipe.

Gently heat the pearl onions in a small saucepan, and add them to the veal.

Strain the cooking liquid, discarding the vegetables. Return the liquid to the kettle, and cook it over high heat until it is reduced to half its original quantity. You should end up with 2 cups of liquid—no more.

Meanwhile, place the mushrooms in a small saucepan with the water, salt, lemon juice, and 1 tablespoon of the butter. Bring to a boil, and simmer gently for 4 minutes.

Remove the saucepan from the heat, and drain the mushrooms, reserving the cooking liquid; add the mushrooms to the veal-onion mixture.

In a medium saucepan, melt 3 tablespoons of the butter over low heat, and add the flour, stirring constantly with a wire whisk.

Add the veal cooking liquid, and bring to a boil; then add the reserved mushroom cooking liquid to the sauce.

Bring the sauce to a boil again, and cook for 15 to 20 minutes, or until the sauce has thickened and has a creamy-smooth texture. (This reduction process is the secret of this marvelous sauce.)

While the sauce is cooking, combine the remaining butter with the egg yolks and sour cream in a small bowl.

Add a small portion of the sauce to this mixture, stirring rapidly; do not allow the egg yolks to curdle.

Return the egg yolk mixture to the remaining sauce, and stir vigorously for 5 minutes over medium heat.

Pour the sauce over the veal mixture, and serve at once with boiled rice.

Serves 6 to 8.

Flour as a thickener yields an opaque sauce that can stand heat for long periods of time without disintegrating.

Cornstarch will dissolve in a liquid more easily than flour, but it is more fragile, and unlike flour, it becomes heavy and gummy when cooked for extended periods of time.

If a flour- or cornstarch-based sauce calls for sugar, never add more than the amount indicated, as excessive amounts will reduce the thickening power of the flour or cornstarch.

Always add acids, such as lemon juice, to the starch mixture after thickening has been completed. If you add it too soon, the sauce may not thicken as well.

When using cornstarch as a thickener, always add a cold, not hot, liquid to the starch.

When thickening any sauce or gravy with flour, cornstarch, or arrowroot, let the mixture cook for at least 5 minutes after the starch has dissolved, so that the sauce won't have a raw starch taste. The mixture will thicken more quickly around the sides and bottom of the saucepan; so you should stir constantly to prevent lumps from forming.

Whatever liquid is thickened with flour or cornstarch must be heated to the boiling point for maximum thickening to occur.

VEAL CORDON BLEU

12 veal scallops, about 3 to 4 ounces each
Salt and pepper to taste
6 slices prosciutto or very thinly sliced boiled ham
6 thin slices Gruyère or Swiss cheese
2 eggs, lightly beaten with 1 teaspoon water
1 cup flour
1½ cups unseasoned bread crumbs
½ cup butter

Place each scallop between two pieces of waxed paper, and pound with a flat mallet or the bottom of a small heavy skillet until the scallops are very thin; sprinkle both sides with salt and pepper to taste .

Place the ham slices in the center of 6 of the scallops; top each with a slice of cheese.

Brush the outside edges of the scallops (around the ham and cheese) with the beaten egg mixture, and top with the remaining 6 scallops.

Carefully dredge the filled pieces of meat in the flour on both sides; dip the pieces in the beaten egg mixture, and then into the bread crumbs until well coated. Pat the pieces with the side of a heavy kitchen knife to help the crumbs adhere.

Transfer the scallops to a wire rack, and refrigerate for 1 to 2 hours, to further enable the coating to adhere.

Melt the butter in a large skillet over medium-high heat, and sauté the cutlets until brown on both sides. Transfer the cutlets to a serving platter, and garnish with parsley sprigs, if desired.

Serves 4 to 6.

Pork & Lamb

ROAST FRESH HAM

Many people, including myself, prefer fresh ham to the smoked variety, because it is less salty. Here is a good basic recipe, which can be easily doubled for larger hams.

1 4-to-5-pound fresh ham
1 tablespoon salt
1 tablespoon paprika
1 tablespoon dry mustard
¼ teaspoon ground ginger

Skin the ham, leaving about ½ inch of fat over the entire surface.

Combine the salt, paprika, mustard, and ginger, and rub the entire ham with this mixture.

Place the ham on a rack in a large roasting pan, and roast at 350°F for 30 to 35 minutes per pound, or until a meat thermometer inserted in the fattest part registers 185°F. (Be sure the ham is completely cooked; it should be grayish-pink and have a delicate aroma.)

A 4-to-5-pound ham will serve 8 to 10.

Note: If desired, midway through cooking time, any of the following glazes can be brushed on the ham to enhance its flavor. Once you brush the ham with one of these glazes, you should continue to brush or baste it every 15 minutes with the pan drippings. A baked, glazed ham can de decorated with fruit slices secured to the meat with toothpicks.

ORANGE HONEY GLAZE

¼ cup prepared mustard
¼ cup orange juice
¼ cup honey
1 tablespoon grated orange peel

Combine all ingredients, and brush on ham.

GRAPE GLAZE

½ cup grape jelly
¼ cup prepared mustard
Dash of ground cloves
Dash of ground cinnamon

Combine all ingredients, and brush on ham.

APRICOT GLAZE

---

1 cup apricot preserves
½ cup honey

Combine the preserves and the honey, and brush on ham.

PINEAPPLE GLAZE

---

1 cup pineapple juice
1 cup brown sugar
1 tablespoon prepared mustard
2 tablespoons lemon juice

Combine all ingredients, and brush on ham.

APPLE GLAZE

---

2 cups apple juice
¾ teaspoon whole allspice
1 teaspoon whole cloves
¼ teaspoon ground ginger
1 cinnamon stick

Combine the juice and spices in a medium saucepan, and bring to a boil over medium heat.

Reduce the heat, and simmer the mixture, covered, for another 5 minutes; strain the mixture, discarding the whole spices.

Baste the ham often with this mixture; about 40 minutes before the end of prescribed baking time, remove the ham from the oven, and brush with the honey. Continue to bake another 30 minutes, or until the ham is shiny.

CHINESE GLAZING SAUCE

This is not only terrific on ham, it's also great for broiled chicken and spareribs.

⅓ cup soy sauce
⅓ cup dry sherry
⅓ cup honey
1 to 2 garlic cloves, crushed
¼ teaspoon Five Chinese Spices (equal parts ground cinnamon, cloves, star anise, fennel, and Szechuan pepper; see Salmon Pâté recipe in Chapter 1)

Mix all of the ingredients together, blending until smooth.

Brush this mixture liberally on the surface of the roast ham; it will give the outside a rich brown glaze.

QUICHE LORRAINE

Although this Swiss cheese pie is most commonly made with bacon, it tastes just as good when made with ham.

PASTRY CRUST:

1 cup flour
Pinch of salt
⅓ cup + 1 tablespoon vegetable shortening
2 to 3 tablespoons ice water

FILLING:

1 tablespoon softened butter or margarine
1 cup grated Swiss cheese
1 cup finely chopped ham
4 eggs
1½ cups heavy cream
¼ teaspoon salt
⅛ teaspoon nutmeg
Pinch of cayenne pepper
Pinch of sugar

To prepare the pastry crust, sift the flour and salt together into a medium bowl.

With a pastry blender or 2 knives, cut in the shortening until the mixture resembles coarse cornmeal.

Gradually add the water, tossing the mixture with a fork, until you can form the dough into a smooth ball.

Turn the dough out onto a lightly floured surface, and with a floured rolling pin, roll the dough into a 12-inch circle.

Carefully fit the dough into a 10-inch fluted quiche pan or a 10-inch pie pan. Chill the dough for 30 minutes.

Preheat the oven to 425°F.

Spread the bottom of the pastry shell with the softened butter. (This seals the pastry shell so that it will not get soggy during baking.)

Sprinkle the Swiss cheese and ham evenly over the pastry shell.

In a medium bowl, beat the eggs with a wire whisk. Add the remaining ingredients, blending well, and pour over the Swiss cheese and ham.

Bake the quiche for 15 minutes. Reduce the oven temperature to 300°F, and continue baking 40 minutes longer, or until a knife inserted in the center comes out clean.

Let the quiche cool on a wire rack for 3 minutes before cutting it into wedges.

Serves 4.

TORTA PRIMAVERA

*I first tasted this fabulous creation in Kansas City, then redis-
covered it in Mission, California. It originated in the Piedmont
region of Italy; let your imagination run free, and concoct your
own variations.*

CRÊPES:

    1¼ cups flour
    1¾ cups milk
    Pinch of salt
    4 eggs
    2 tablespoons melted butter
    Additional melted butter for making crêpes

FILLING:

    2 packages (10 ounces each) frozen chopped spinach,
        thawed and drained of all liquid
    2 tablespoons butter
    ¼ teaspoon garlic powder
    Salt and pepper to taste
    1 cup mayonnaise (approximately)
    ½ pound Genoa salami, sliced paper-thin
    ½ pound provolone cheese, sliced paper-thin
    3 hard-boiled eggs, sliced paper-thin
    ½ pound Danish ham or prosciutto, sliced paper-thin

A few hours before serving, prepare the crêpe batter: Combine the flour, milk, salt, eggs, and 2 tablespoons of melted
butter in a blender container or a food processor. Blend or
process until the batter is very smooth. Refrigerate the batter,
covered, for at least 2 hours.

Meanwhile, prepare the spinach filling: in a large skillet,
sauté the thawed spinach in the butter until it is very dry.
Season with the garlic powder, and salt and pepper to taste;
allow the mixture to cool to room temperature.

To make the crêpes, heat a 7- or 8-inch crêpe pan over medium heat for 3 minutes; brush with some melted butter.

Using a ladle or small measuring cup, add about 2 to 3 tablespoons of the batter to the pan. Immediately tilt the pan to cover the bottom evenly with the batter.

Cook until the batter appears dry on top and is golden brown underneath; with a flexible spatula, turn the crêpe, and cook it about 10 seconds longer on the other side.

Slide the crêpe onto a wire rack, and repeat the process, brushing the pan with melted butter about every other crêpe. Stack the crêpes on top of one another, and keep them moist with a damp towel. You will have about 18 crêpes.

To assemble the dish: Spread one crêpe lightly with mayonnaise, and arrange a layer of the salami.

Top with another crêpe, and spread with some of the spinach filling.

Place the next crêpe on top, spread it with some mayonnaise, and arrange some of the cheese slices on top. The next crêpe should be spread with some of the spinach filling. Continue this procedure, using the sliced eggs and the ham, alternating them with the spinach filling. Then repeat the layers with the salami and cheese, and continue until all the crêpes and fillings are used up.

Ice the top crêpe with the remaining mayonnaise, and decorate with sliced pimiento or olives, if desired. To serve, cut into wedges.

Serves 4.

TOSTADAS FANG

These open-faced sandwiches remind me of a snowcapped Mexican mountain on a plate.

---

1 large head Iceberg lettuce, thinly sliced
1 bunch scallions, chopped
½ pound Monterey Jack cheese, grated
1 pound chorizo (Mexican sausage—available at most markets)
1 can (1 pound) Mexican-style refried beans
¼ to ½ cup salad oil
4 large (8 to 10 inches in diameter) flour tortillas
1 cup commercial medium-mild red taco sauce
Optional for garnish: 4 tomatoes cut in wedges; avocado wedges; chopped ripe olives; julienne slices of turkey or chicken
1 to 2 pints sour cream
Paprika

In a large chilled bowl, combine the lettuce, scallions, and the cheese; cover and refrigerate.

Remove the chorizo from its casing, and in a large skillet cook the meat until it is brown and crumbly.

Add the beans, and cook, stirring for another few minutes. Remove the mixture from the heat, and keep it warm.

Preheat the oven to 140°F, and heat 4 large plates for serving.

In another skillet, heat about ½ inch of oil until it is very hot, and fry the tortillas, one at a time, until they are golden-brown and crisp.

Drain the tortillas well on paper towels.

Transfer the tortillas to the plates in the oven if not serving right away.

To serve, remove the tortillas and the plates from the oven, and spread equal amounts of the chorizo-bean mixture over each one.

Toss the lettuce, scallions, and cheese with the taco sauce, and heap this mixture on top of the chorizo-bean mixture.

Arrange any or all of the optional garnish ingredients on each side of the "mountain," and top with the sour cream, letting it run down the sides.

Finish with a flourish of paprika, and . . . viva!

Serves 4.

LAMB RAGOUT

A marvelous one-pot dish that needs only a tossed salad and perhaps a loaf of French bread to turn it into a very satisfying company meal.

¼ cup flour
1 teaspoon salt
Freshly ground pepper to taste
2½ pounds shoulder of lamb, cut into 1½-inch cubes
3 tablespoons bacon fat (oil can be substituted)
1 garlic clove, crushed
2 medium onions, coarsely chopped
2 stalks celery, chopped
1 carrot, chopped
½ cup chopped mushrooms
1 cup long grain raw white rice
2 tomatoes, peeled and coarsely chopped
1 bay leaf
½ teaspoon oregano
1 cup beef or chicken broth
1 cup dry white wine
2 tablespoons chopped parsley

Combine the flour, salt, and pepper in a paper or plastic bag; add the cubed lamb, and shake the bag vigorously to dredge the meat with the flour.

In a heavy skillet over medium-high heat, melt the bacon fat, and sauté the lamb until brown on all sides; transfer the meat to a large casserole as it browns.

Preheat the oven to 325°F.

To the fat remaining in the skillet, add the garlic, onion, celery, carrot, and mushrooms; sauté very lightly until the vegetables show just a trace of brown.

Add the vegetables to the casserole, and in the same skillet, lightly brown the rice, adding a little more fat if necessary.

Add the rice to the casserole, along with the tomato, bay leaf, and the oregano.

Pour the stock and the wine into the skillet, to deglaze it by scraping up any browned bits that have adhered to the bottom; add this to the casserole, cover it tightly, and bake for 1½ hours, or until the meat is very tender and the rice has absorbed all the liquid.

If the rice has not absorbed all the liquid, remove the cover, and let the casserole bake another 15 minutes.

Discard the bay leaf, and correct the seasonings before serving the dish garnished with the parsley.

Serves 6.

KOOFTAH CURRY

Serve these curried meatballs over boiled white rice, or make hearty sandwiches by filling pita (pocket) bread with the mixture. The ideal accompaniment is peach chutney.

1½ pounds ground lamb
1 small onion, finely chopped
2 teaspoons salt
¼ teaspoon cinnamon
⅛ teaspoon ground cloves
1 egg, lightly beaten
¼ cup salad oil
1 medium onion, thinly sliced
2 teaspoons curry powder
2 tablespoons tomato paste
1 cup water

In a medium bowl, combine the lamb, chopped onion, 1 teaspoon of the salt, cinnamon, cloves, and the beaten egg. Form into 1- or 2-inch meatballs, and set aside.

Heat 2 tablespoons of the oil in a large skillet, and sauté the sliced onion until it is lightly browned; remove the onion slices, and set them aside.

Add the remaining oil to the skillet, and cook the meatballs over medium heat until they are brown on all sides.

Add the sliced onions, the remaining salt, the curry powder, tomato paste, and the water to the skillet; cook the mixture, covered, for 20 minutes.

Serve the meatballs with rice or pita bread, with peach chutney on the side.

Serves 4.

Chicken

LEMON ROASTED CAPON

A recipe from Sara Sharpe, a great Florida caterer and teacher.

1 6-pound capon
Salt and pepper
2 or 3 lemons, thinly sliced
1 large onion, cut into chunks
½ cup fresh chopped parsley
1 teaspoon tarragon
2 tablespoons melted butter or margarine
¼ cup dry Madeira
4 medium onions, quartered

Preheat the oven to 375°F.

Rinse the capon, dry it with paper towels, and rub it inside and out with the salt and pepper.

Carefully slip the lemon slices between the skin and the flesh everywhere you can; do not crowd the slices.

If there are any slices left, place them in the chest cavity, along with 4 chunks of the onion, the parsley, and the tarragon.

Tie the legs together, secure the wing tips, and place the bird, breast side down, in a large roasting pan.

Combine the melted butter with the Madeira, and brush it all over the skin of the capon.

Roast the capon for 30 minutes; turn it breast side up, and roast it for another hour, basting frequently with the pan drippings. If the capon appears to be browning too quickly, cover it lightly with aluminum foil.

Scatter the remaining onion chunks in the roasting pan, and roast the capon for another half hour. The capon should be done after 2 hours. To test for doneness, the juices should run clear when the thigh is pricked with a fork.

Serves 4 to 6.

HINTS ON ONION SELECTION

Bermuda—large with flattened shape and yellow skin; mild, delicate flavor.

Italian—red onion, mild and sweet; good for salads and garnishes.

Pearl—small, round, about the size of a pea; used for garnish or served pickled as a condiment.

Spanish—large, yellow-skinned, mild flavored.

Green—small, with crisp green tops; also called chives. Very similar to spring onions, which are also known as scallions.

Shallots—small bulb under a dry, reddish-brown outer skin; mild flavor is somewhere between that of an onion and garlic.

White—small, with pure white outer skin; these onions are always cooked and served whole in stews such as Boeuf Bourguignon.

Yellow—the most common variety of all; these are usually small to medium in size.

The best onions are clean and firm, with dry, smooth skins. Avoid onions with wet, soggy necks or with soft, spongy bulbs. Store onions in a dry, cool, well-ventilated area; it should not be too warm or too cold.

CHICKEN BREASTS DIVINE

This is turning into everyone's favorite dinner-party entrée.

2 tablespoons Worcestershire sauce
2 pints whipping cream
¾ cup mango chutney, cut into small pieces
6 whole chicken breasts, cut in half
¼ cup corn oil
Salt and freshly ground pepper to taste

In the top part of a double boiler, over simmering water, combine the Worcestershire sauce, the whipping cream, and the chutney; cover, and cook, stirring occasionally, for 1½ hours.

Meanwhile, preheat the oven to 350°F.

Brush the chicken with the oil, and sprinkle with salt and pepper to taste.

Place the chicken, skin side up, in a large shallow baking pan, and bake for about 45 minutes, or until the meat is almost done.

Reduce the oven temperature to 300°F, and pour the sauce over the chicken breasts; cook for another 15 to 20 minutes.

Serve with boiled white rice.

Serves 6.

CHICKEN JOSEPHINE

Also known as chicken piccata, this dish is from Josephine's, one of my favorite New York restaurants.

---

4 whole chicken breasts, skinned, boned, and halved
½ cup flour
Salt and freshly ground pepper to taste
2 teaspoons paprika
¼ cup clarified butter (melt about 4½ tablespoons of
    butter, and skim off the milky residue)
1 tablespoon olive oil
3 tablespoons dry Madeira
3 or 4 tablespoons fresh lemon juice
¼ cup fresh minced parsley

Place each chicken breast half between 2 sheets of waxed paper, and, using a cleaver or the handle of a chef's knife, pound it until it is thin.

Mix together the flour, salt, and pepper to taste, and the paprika.

Place the flour mixture in a paper or plastic bag, and add the chicken breasts, a few at a time, shaking to coat them lightly.

Heat the butter and oil in a large skillet until they are bubbly, and sauté the breasts for 3 to 5 minutes on each side; drain the pieces, and keep them warm.

Drain off all but 2 tablespoons of the fat in the skillet, and add the Madeira; stir well, scraping up any pieces of meat or coating sticking to the skillet.

Add the lemon juice to taste, and cook until the sauce thickens slightly; add the parsley, and pour the sauce over the chicken.

Serves 4 to 6.

CHICKEN BREASTS STUFFED WITH SAUSAGE

A new combination that will draw raves.

¼ cup butter or margarine
¾ pound fresh mushrooms, sliced
2 medium onions, chopped
1 cup chopped celery
1 pound hot Italian sausage, removed from casing
Salt and pepper to taste
½ cup fresh bread crumbs
4 chicken breasts, boned and halved
Corn oil

In a large skillet, melt the butter, and sauté the mushrooms, onions, and celery for about 3 minutes.

Preheat the oven to 350°F.

Add the sausage to the skillet, and cook another 5 minutes; season with salt and pepper to taste.

Place the contents of the skillet in a blender container or a food processor.

Add the bread crumbs, and blend or process for 30 seconds, or just until the mixture is finely chopped and blended.

Place each chicken breast half skin side down, and place about 3 tablespoons of the stuffing in the center of each piece.

Fold the chicken breast half in thirds, and secure it with toothpicks.

Place the chicken breasts, folded side down, in a baking dish, and brush each breast with the corn oil.

Bake for 30 to 45 minutes, or until the chicken is tender.

Serves 4 to 6.

CHICKEN KIEV

A fabulous new version of a classic dish, this comes from a fellow cooking enthusiast in New Jersey.

---

4 whole chicken breasts, skinned, boned, and cut in half
1 cup butter, softened
8 ounces cream cheese
1 cup grated cheddar cheese
½ cup grated Parmesan cheese
¼ cup chopped parsley
¼ cup chopped chives
2 tablespoons minced shallots
⅓ cup sliced blanched almonds
½ teaspoon freshly ground pepper
Pinch of salt
1 cup flour seasoned with salt and pepper to taste
6 eggs, well beaten
1 cup bread crumbs seasoned with 2 tablespoons grated
   Parmesan cheese
Oil for deep frying

Using a meat cleaver or the handle of a chef's knife, pound out the chicken breasts.

In a small bowl, combine the butter, the 3 cheeses, the parsley, chives, shallots, almonds, pepper, and the salt.

Place about 3 tablespoons of this mixture in the center of each chicken breast half; roll the meat around the filling, and secure with toothpicks.

Dip the breasts in the seasoned flour, and refrigerate for 3 to 4 hours.

Dip the breasts in the beaten eggs, and then in the seasoned bread crumbs, coating well.

In a large skillet or an electric skillet with a thermostat, heat about 2 cups of oil to 350°F, and cook the chicken for about 20 minutes, turning often, until it is thoroughly cooked; drain on paper towels briefly before serving.

If not being served right away, the chicken can be individually wrapped and frozen after it completely cools. Reheat the frozen chicken by placing it directly from the freezer, still wrapped in foil, into a 400°F oven for about 25 minutes.

Serves 6 to 8.

NUTTY CHICKEN

---

8 whole chicken breasts, skinned, boned, and split in half
Salt and freshly ground pepper to taste
½ cup lemon juice
2 cups sour cream
½ teaspoon garlic powder
2 teaspoons celery salt
2 teaspoons paprika
2 cups ground walnuts (use blender or food processor)
1 cup melted butter or margarine
½ cup dry white wine

The day before serving, place the chicken breast halves in 1 or 2 large bowls, and season them with salt and pepper to taste.

Add ¼ cup of the lemon juice, and let the breasts stand for 1½ hours.

Combine the sour cream with the remaining lemon juice, and add the garlic powder, celery salt, and the paprika.

Coat the chicken with the sour cream mixture, and refrigerate, covered, overnight.

The next day, preheat the oven to 350°F.

Roll the chicken breasts in the ground walnuts, coating well; place the pieces in a large, well-greased baking dish.

Spoon ½ cup of the melted butter over the chicken, and bake for 30 minutes.

Combine the remaining butter with the wine, and use this mixture to baste the chicken, baking it for another 10 minutes.

Serves 8.

CHICKEN NIÇOISE

I first tasted this in my favorite French restaurant in Washington, D.C., and I subsequently experimented until I came up with a close facsimile.

6 whole chicken breasts, skinned and boned
6 thin slices baked ham
3 ripe bananas, sliced in half lengthwise
3 tablespoons melted butter or margarine
⅔ cup bread crumbs
2 cups orange juice
2 tablespoons grated orange peel
1 tablespoon sugar
1 teaspoon curry powder

Preheat the oven to 400°F.

Open each chicken breast out in butterfly fashion; place a slice of ham and banana half on one half of each breast; fold it in half, and secure with toothpicks.

Lay the chicken breasts in a large baking dish, and brush them with the butter; sprinkle them with the bread crumbs.

Bake, uncovered, for 15 minutes.

While the chicken is baking, combine the remaining ingredients in a small saucepan, and simmer over low heat for 5 minutes. Correct the seasoning if necessary.

Reduce the oven temperature to 350°F, and pour the sauce over the breasts; cover the baking dish, and bake for 30 minutes longer.

Remove the toothpicks before serving, and serve with boiled white rice.

Serves 6.

CHICKEN MOUTARDE

A splendid company dish that will leave no doubt about your cooking finesse!

---

3 tablespoons Dijon mustard
½ cup dry white wine
1½ teaspoons Worcestershire sauce
4 whole chicken breasts, skinned, boned, and halved
2 cups unseasoned bread crumbs
½ cup unsalted butter
¼ cup dry mustard
1 tablespoon water
¼ cup finely chopped shallots
1 tablespoon white wine vinegar
Freshly ground pepper to taste
1 bay leaf
¼ teaspoon thyme
2 cups whipping cream

In a shallow bowl, combine the mustard, 3 tablespoons of the wine, and the Worcestershire sauce.

Dip each chicken breast half in this mixture, and then in the bread crumbs.

Melt the butter in a large skillet over low heat, and sauté the chicken breasts, turning several times, until they are thoroughly cooked. Remove the meat to a shallow dish, and keep warm in a slow (200°F) oven.

Combine the dry mustard with the water, and set aside.

In the same skillet, sauté the chopped shallots for 1 or 2 minutes; if more butter is needed, add another tablespoon.

Add the remaining white wine, the vinegar, pepper, bay leaf, and thyme.

Cook, stirring, over medium-high heat until most of the liquid has evaporated.

Stir in the whipping cream, and cook over medium heat until the mixture is thick—about 10 minutes.

Add the mustard-water mixture, mixing well. Discard the bay leaf.

Pour the sauce over the chicken, and serve with lots of sliced French bread to mop up the extra sauce.

Serves 4.

SOYAU CHICKEN

1½ cups soy sauce
3 cups water
1 cup dark brown sugar
2 tablespoons honey
1 tablespoon dry sherry
4 whole chicken breasts, skinned and boned

In a large kettle, combine the soy sauce, water, sugar, honey, and the sherry.

Slowly cook this mixture over medium heat for 10 minutes; then turn the heat up, and bring the mixture to a boil.

Meanwhile, cut the chicken breasts into strips about 2 to 3 inches long and 1½ inches wide.

Add the chicken pieces to the sauce; cover the kettle, reduce the heat, and simmer the mixture for about 30 minutes, or until the chicken is tender.

Serve the chicken in the sauce, hot or cold, with boiled white rice.

Serves 6 to 8.

CHICKEN SZECHUAN WITH CASHEWS

Szechuan cooking is very highly seasoned, but this recipe is a good introduction, since it is spicy without being overly hot.

---

2 whole chicken breasts, skinned and boned
1 tablespoon cornstarch
Pinch of salt
1 tablespoon dry sherry
1 tablespoon sesame oil
1 tablespoon bean sauce
1 tablespoon hoisin sauce
1 tablespoon soy sauce
1 teaspoon vinegar
½ teaspoon garlic powder
3 to 4 tablespoons peanut oil
1 teaspoon minced ginger root
½ cup roasted unsalted cashews

Cut the chicken into thin strips.

Prepare a marinade by combining the cornstarch, salt, sherry, and sesame oil in a medium bowl; marinate the chicken in this mixture for 1 or more hours.

Combine the bean sauce, hoisin sauce, soy sauce, vinegar, and the garlic powder in a small bowl; set aside.

Heat 3 tablespoons of peanut oil in a wok over medium-high heat; stir in the ginger, and cook for about 10 seconds.

Add the chicken (with its marinade), and stir-fry continuously until the meat is cooked—about 5 minutes. Add more oil if necessary.

Add the bean sauce mixture and one-half of the cashews; mix quickly, and transfer the mixture to a serving platter.

Garnish the mixture with the remaining cashews, and serve with boiled white rice.

Serves 2 to 4.

AFRICAN CHICKEN

A North African version of the popular Mexican dish, Chicken Mole.

---

1 3½- to 4-pound roasting chicken
Salt and freshly ground pepper
½ cup slivered blanched almonds
3 tablespoons butter or margarine
2 teaspoons curry powder
1 medium tomato, peeled and coarsely chopped
1 cup cooked white rice
½ cup seedless yellow raisins
1½ tablespoons finely chopped parsley
½ teaspoon cinnamon
½ ounce unsweetened chocolate, grated

Preheat the oven to 375°F.

Sprinkle the chicken inside and out with salt and pepper.

In a small skillet, sauté the almonds in 1 tablespoon of the butter until they are golden.

Stir in the curry powder, cook another minute, and remove from the heat.

Add the tomato, rice, raisins, parsley, cinnamon, and the chocolate, plus a little salt and pepper to taste; mix well.

Use this mixture to stuff the chest and neck cavities of the chicken; secure the openings with skewers; truss the wings and the legs.

Rub the outside of the chicken with the remaining butter, and roast for 1½ to 1¾ hours, or until the chicken is tender; baste occasionally with the pan juices.

Serves 4.

Basting with butter adds flavor to poultry and helps give the skin a rich brown coating.

Dry and liquid measures are not the same. A dry pint is 33.6 cubic inches, and a liquid pint is 28.875 cubic inches. So it's best not to use a Pyrex or liquid measuring cup (with a pouring lip) for dry ingredients, or a metal measuring cup for liquids.

CHICKEN NORMANDY STYLE

The modifier "Normandy" usually indicates that the recipe contains brandy or cognac, for which the Normandy region of France is noted.

½ cup butter or margarine
1 3-pound frying chicken, cut into 8 pieces
2 medium onions, peeled and thinly sliced
Salt and freshly ground pepper to taste
2 tablespoons flour
1½ teaspoons curry powder (or to taste)
1 cup whipping cream
⅓ cup brandy

Melt the butter in a heavy skillet over medium-high heat, and add the chicken pieces, the onion, and salt and pepper to taste.

Reduce the heat, and cook the chicken, tightly covered, for about 35 minutes, or until it is fork-tender; remove the chicken to a heated platter, and keep it warm.

Combine the flour and curry powder, and add this mixture to the butter and onions in the skillet, stirring over low heat until smooth.

Stir in the cream and the brandy, and cook over low heat, stirring constantly, until the sauce is thickened and smooth.

Return the chicken to the sauce, and simmer gently for 10 minutes.

Serve the chicken with the sauce over boiled white rice.

Serves 4.

CHICKEN CRÊPES

CRÊPE BATTER:

3 eggs
1½ cups milk
1½ cups flour
1 teaspoon melted butter
Additional melted butter for cooking crêpes

CHICKEN & STOCK:

1 3-pound frying or roasting chicken (including giblets)
1 tablespoon salt
12 peppercorns
1 onion, peeled and stuck with 2 cloves
1 large carrot, sliced
Some celery leaves
1 bay leaf

VELOUTÉ SAUCE:

¼ cup butter or margarine
6 tablespoons flour
2 cups reserved chicken stock
2 cups table cream or half-and-half
Salt and freshly ground pepper
Pinch of nutmeg
2 cups grated Swiss cheese

Several hours before serving, prepare the crêpe batter: combine the eggs, milk, flour, and melted butter in a blender container or food processor; blend or process until the batter is smooth. Then let it stand at room temperature for 2 hours.

Meanwhile, cook the chicken: place the chicken in a large kettle with the giblets, salt, peppercorns, onion, carrot, celery leaves, and the bay leaf.

Add enough water to cover the chicken, and bring to a boil; reduce the heat, and simmer, covered, for 1 hour, or until the meat falls off the bone.

When the chicken is cool enough to handle, remove it from the pot; strain and reserve the stock. (You will need 2 cups for the Velouté Sauce; the remainder can be frozen for future use.)

Remove the skin and bones from the chicken, and cut the meat into small pieces; you should have about 3 cups of chicken. Set it aside.

To make the crêpes, heat a 7- or 8-inch crêpe pan for 3 minutes over medium-high heat.

Brush the pan with some melted butter, and using a ladle or measuring cup, add about 2 to 3 tablespoons of the batter; quickly rotate the pan to cover the bottom (not sides) of the pan evenly with the batter.

Let the crêpe cook until it is dry on top and lightly browned underneath—about 30 seconds. Turn the crêpe with a flexible spatula, and cook it for about 10 seconds longer.

Slide the crêpe onto a wire rack, and repeat the procedure, brushing the pan with melted butter about every other crêpe. Continue to stack the crêpes on top of one another. You should have about 16 to 18 crêpes.

To prepare the Velouté Sauce, melt the butter in a medium saucepan, and with a wire whisk, stir in the flour, mixing until smooth.

Remove the saucepan from the heat, and gradually add the reserved chicken stock, stirring with a wire whisk.

Return the saucepan to medium heat, and cook, stirring, for about 15 minutes.

Add the cream and the seasonings, and cook 5 minutes longer; remove from the heat.

To assemble the crêpes, combine about one half of the Velouté Sauce with the chicken in a medium bowl; add 1 cup of the grated cheese.

Place 2 to 3 tablespoons of the chicken mixture in the center of each crêpe. Fold the crêpe in thirds, and place it, seam side down, in a large, shallow, well-greased baking dish. Repeat with the remaining crêpes and filling.

Pour the remaining sauce over the filled crêpes, and sprinkle with the remaining cheese. (At this point, the dish may be frozen or refrigerated until needed.)

About 40 minutes before serving, preheat the oven to 375°F.

Bake crêpes, uncovered, until the sauce is bubbly and the topping is golden brown. (If you are baking the crêpes directly from the freezer, increase the baking time to 45 minutes.)

Serves 6 to 8.

Note: You can also combine chopped cooked spinach, mushrooms, or onions with the chicken to create different fillings.

CHICKEN LASAGNE

A popular entrée with a new twist—chicken is used instead of ground beef.

---

1 large onion, chopped
⅓ cup olive oil
½ teaspoon garlic powder
½ pound chicken livers, chopped
¼ pound prosciutto, chopped
2 cups diced cooked chicken
2 cans (1 pound each) herbed tomato sauce
2 cans (6 ounces each) tomato paste
1 cup canned or homemade chicken broth
1 cup dry white wine
Pinch of salt
Freshly ground pepper to taste
½ teaspoon basil
½ teaspoon oregano
1 package (1 pound) lasagne
1 pound ricotta cheese
2 cups grated Parmesan cheese
½ pound mozzarella cheese, sliced

In a large kettle, sauté the onion in the olive oil over medium heat for about 3 minutes.

Add the garlic powder and the chicken livers, and sauté until the livers are browned.

Add the prosciutto, chicken, tomato sauce, tomato paste, chicken broth, wine, and the seasonings.

Bring the mixture to a boil; reduce the heat, and simmer, covered, for 30 minutes. Stir occasionally during this period.

Meanwhile, prepare the lasagne according to the package directions; rinse with cold water, and drain.

Preheat the oven to 350° F.

Pour a little of the sauce into a 16 × 9 × 2½-inch lasagne pan or rectangular baking dish.

Spread with a layer of lasagne, overlapping the pieces; spread the lasagne with one-third of the ricotta, and sprinkle with one-third of the Parmesan cheese. Spoon more sauce over the cheese.

Make 2 more layers, using the ingredients in this order: lasagne, ricotta, Parmesan, and sauce. Arrange the mozzarella slices over the last layer of sauce.

Bake the lasagne, uncovered, for 30 minutes, or until the sauce is bubbly. Let the dish stand for 10 minutes before cutting it into squares.

Serves 10.

Fish & Seafood

SOLE VERONIQUE

1 pound fresh mushrooms, sliced
10 tablespoons butter or margarine
Salt and freshly ground pepper to taste
2 pounds fillets of sole
1 cup milk
¾ pound seedless green grapes
½ cup table cream
1½ tablespoons flour
½ cup grated Parmesan cheese

Preheat the oven to 400°F.

In a large skillet, sauté the mushrooms in 6 tablespoons of the butter; season with salt and pepper to taste, and cook for 3 minutes. Remove from the heat, and set aside.

In a large saucepan over medium heat, poach the sole fillets in gently simmering milk for 6 to 7 minutes.

Carefully remove the sole with a slotted spoon, and drain the fillets on paper towels; reserve the milk.

Place one-third of the fillets in a large casserole, and top them with one-third of the mushrooms and one-third of the grapes. Make 2 more layers of sole, mushrooms, and grapes.

Melt the remaining butter in a medium saucepan over low heat, and stir in the flour with a wire whisk; cook for 2 minutes, making sure the mixture does not brown.

Add the reserved milk, and cook, stirring, until the mixture is smooth and thickened; add the cream, and one-half of the Parmesan cheese.

Pour the sauce over the fish-mushroom-grape layers, and sprinkle with the remaining Parmesan cheese.

Bake, uncovered, for 15 minutes, or until the sauce is bubbly and golden brown on top.

Serves 4 to 6.

SIMPLY DELICIOUS FISH

Pinch of salt
½ teaspoon freshly ground pepper
½ teaspoon garlic powder
2 pounds fish fillets (flounder, sole, haddock)
½ cup melted butter or margarine
3 tablespoons lemon juice
¼ cup soy sauce
3 tablespoons chopped fresh parsley

Preheat the oven to 350°F.

Combine the salt, pepper, and garlic powder, and rub the fish fillets with this mixture.

Place the fillets in a single layer in a large, shallow, lightly greased baking dish, and bake them for 10 minutes.

Combine the melted butter with the lemon juice and soy sauce; pour one-half of this mixture over the fish, and bake for 20 minutes longer.

Just before serving, pour the remaining sauce over the fish, and garnish with the parsley. Serve with boiled white rice.

Serves 4 to 6.

HINT

If fish is dry, such as haddock, cod, or flounder, you can serve it with a rich sauce, containing some fat; a fatty fish, such as salmon or mackerel, goes best with tomato, dill, or caper sauce.

---

2 pounds fish fillets (sole, halibut, or flounder)
¼ cup butter or margarine
Salt and freshly ground pepper to taste
1 teaspoon paprika
¼ cup orange or lime marmalade
¼ cup smooth or chunky peanut butter
2 teaspoons lemon juice
2 tablespoons minced parsley

Preheat the oven to Broil.

Place the fish on a lightly greased broiler pan, and dot with the butter.

Sprinkle the fish with the salt, pepper, and the paprika, and broil it for 5 minutes.

While the fish is broiling, combine the remaining ingredients in a small bowl.

Remove the fish from the oven, and with a spatula, spread the marmalade mixture over the fish.

Return the pan to the oven, and broil until the fish flakes easily when it is poked with a fork—about 5 minutes.

Serves 4.

HINT

Hungarian paprika, which is usually sold only in gourmet specialty shops, is sweeter than Spanish paprika, the kind most commonly found on supermarket shelves.

FLOUNDER Á L'ITALIENNE

2 pounds flounder fillets
Paprika
½ cup butter or margarine
3 tablespoons salad oil
Salt and freshly ground pepper to taste
½ teaspoon oregano
1 teaspoon lemon juice
⅓ cup dry white wine
½ cup unseasoned bread crumbs

Preheat the oven to 350°F.

Place the fillets in a large, shallow, lightly greased baking dish, and sprinkle them with some paprika.

Melt the butter in a medium saucepan over medium heat; add the oil, spices, lemon juice, and the wine.

Cook the mixture just until thoroughly heated, and pour over the fish.

Sprinkle the bread crumbs on top, and bake, uncovered, for 30 to 35 minutes, or until the fish flakes easily when poked with a fork.

Serve with boiled white rice or pasta.

Serves 4.

HINT

If you are cooking fish fillets with the skin on, place them skin side down about 2 inches from the source of heat. Baste them as they cook, but you do not have to turn them. Whole fish or very large fillets that are going to be broiled should be placed about 6 inches from the broiler and cooked for about 6 minutes (or longer) per side, turning at least once.

BAKED SNAPPER

2 pounds fillet of red snapper
¼ cup grated Parmesan cheese
¼ cup sour cream
¼ cup mayonnaise
Salt and freshly ground pepper to taste
3 scallions, sliced
1 tablespoon red wine vinegar
Dash of Tabasco sauce

Preheat the oven to 350°F.

Place the fillets in a large, shallow, lightly greased baking dish.

In a small bowl, combine the cheese, sour cream, and mayonnaise; add some salt and pepper to taste.

Add the remaining ingredients, mixing well.

Spoon this mixture over the fish fillets, and bake, uncovered, for 25 to 30 minutes, or until the fish flakes easily when poked with a fork.

Serves 4.

HINT

When buying fresh whole fish, the eyes should be clear and bright, not milky. The skin should feel firm and springy when pressed. There should be a pleasant, not strong, odor, and the gills should be reddish or pink.

LASAGNE, SEAFOOD STYLE

This might be one of the most caloric dishes you've ever tasted —also one of the most unique!

---

8 to 10 lasagne noodles
3 tablespoons butter or margarine
¾ pound mushrooms, sliced
2 packages (8 ounces each) cream cheese, softened
1½ cups cottage cheese
1 pint whipping or table cream
1 egg
2 teaspoons fresh basil, crumbled (or 1 teaspoon dried
   basil)
¼ teaspoon salt
Pinch of white pepper
1 pound shrimp, cooked and peeled
1 pound crabmeat, flaked
¼ cup grated Parmesan cheese
¾ cup cheddar cheese

Cook the lasagne according to the package directions; rinse in cold water, and drain well.

Meanwhile, melt the butter in a large skillet over medium heat, and sauté the mushrooms until they are tender.

Remove from the heat, and blend in the cream cheese, cottage cheese, cream, egg, basil, salt and pepper.

Place one-half of the lasagne on the bottom of a 9 × 13 × 2-inch baking dish; top with half of the shrimp and half of the crabmeat.

Spread one-half of the cream cheese mixture over the seafood; repeat the layers using the remaining ingredients.

Sprinkle the Parmesan on top of the last layer. (The dish may be prepared in advance up to this point, and frozen or refrigerated until needed.)

About 1¼ hours before serving, preheat the oven to 350°F.

Bake the lasagne, uncovered, for 40 to 45 minutes; sprinkle the cheddar cheese on top, and bake 3 minutes longer.

Let the baking dish stand at room temperature for 15 minutes before cutting into squares.

Serves 12.

SHRIMP KABOBS

Serve this over a bed of white rice, accompanied by a tossed green salad.

---

2 pounds medium-size raw shrimp
¾ pound mushrooms
1½ cups beer
½ cup soy sauce
1 teaspoon garlic powder
1 pint cherry tomatoes
3 green peppers, cut into 2-inch squares

Shell and devein the shrimp.

Brush the mushroom caps to remove any dirt; remove the stems, and set them aside for use in another recipe.

Combine the beer, soy sauce, and garlic powder in a medium bowl, and marinate the shrimp and the mushrooms in this mixture for 2 to 3 hours.

Drain off the marinade, and reserve it.

Preheat the oven to Broil, or heat charcoal on an outdoor grill.

Divide the mushrooms and the shrimp evenly among 6 to 8 skewers, and thread them alternately with the tomatoes and green pepper.

Broil or grill the kabobs approximately 5 minutes on each side, brushing often with the reserved marinade.

Serves 6 to 8.

SHRIMP KIEV

---

24 large raw shrimp, shelled and deveined
½ cup dry white wine
1 stick unsalted butter, cut into 24 1-inch fingers and
   frozen
Juice of 1 lemon
Freshly ground salt and pepper
2 tablespoons finely chopped fresh chives
½ cup flour
4 eggs, beaten with 2 tablespoons of salad oil
2 cups fresh bread crumbs
Oil for deep frying

Cut the shrimp lengthwise along the concave side, but do not cut completely through.

Sprinkle a sheet of waxed paper with the wine, and spread the shrimp open (butterfly fashion) on the paper.

Cover the shrimp with another sheet of waxed paper, and pound the shrimp with a meat cleaver or the handle of a large chef's knife; the shrimp should be very thin.

Remove the upper sheet of paper, and brush each shrimp with the wine.

Lay a finger of frozen butter in the center of each shrimp; sprinkle with lemon juice, salt and pepper to taste, and ¼ teaspoon of the chives.

Roll the shrimp up, tucking in the ends; secure them with toothpicks.

Place the flour, the egg-oil mixture, and the bread crumbs in 3 separate bowls.

Dip the shrimp first in the flour, then in the egg mixture, and finally in the bread crumbs.

Place the shrimp in a dish, seam side down, and freeze them for at least 1 hour before cooking. (They can be frozen for up to 4 days.)

Heat at least 2 inches of oil in a deep fat fryer or an electric skillet to 375°F.

Fry the frozen shrimp, seam side down, a few at a time for 5 minutes; drain them quickly on paper towels, and serve hot.

Serves 4.

SHRIMP CURRY IN THE FRENCH MANNER

Mild and subtle.

¼ cup butter or margarine
1 medium onion, finely chopped
3 to 4 teaspoons curry powder
2½ pounds raw shrimp, shelled and deveined
2 cups whipping cream
Pinch of salt
Freshly ground pepper to taste
Pinch of cayenne
1 egg yolk

In a large skillet, melt the butter over medium heat, and sauté the onion until it is soft and yellow.

Add the curry powder, and stir well; cook over low heat for 1 minute.

Add the shrimp, and toss them well, adding more butter if the pan is too dry.

Cook the shrimp over low heat for 2 to 3 minutes.

Add 1 cup of the cream, and cook over medium heat for 5 minutes, stirring frequently; remove the shrimp with a slotted spoon, and keep them warm.

Continue cooking the cream mixture until it begins to thicken slightly.

Stir in another ½ cup of the cream, and the seasonings; cook for a few minutes longer to blend and reduce the sauce slightly.

In a small bowl, mix the egg yolk with the remaining cream.

Remove the skillet from the heat, and allow the sauce to cool slightly.

Stir in the egg yolk–cream mixture, beating with a wire whisk.

Return the skillet to low heat, and add the shrimp; cook only until the shrimp are hot and the sauce is slightly thickened, stirring gently the entire time.

Do not let the sauce come to a boil or get too hot, as the egg yolk will curdle the sauce.

Correct the seasonings, and serve the dish over boiled white rice.

Serves 6.

SCAMPI BREAD

Like most shrimp entrées, this one is rather expensive, but it makes an ideal main course for a fancy luncheon or a midnight supper. Or, if you're pulling out all the stops, serve it as a prelude to a very elegant dinner.

---

12 small individual French bread rolls, cut in half
   lengthwise
1 pound butter or margarine, softened
½ cup finely chopped parsley
2 tablespoons finely chopped shallots
1 to 2 teaspoons garlic powder
¼ teaspoon basil
1 teaspoon salt
2 tablespoons ground blanched almonds
1¾ pounds raw shrimp, peeled
1 to 2 tablespoons pickling spices
¾ cup dry white wine

Preheat the oven to 400°F.

Hollow out the rolls, placing the removed bread into a food processor or blender container; process or blend to make bread crumbs, and set them aside.

In the food processor or blender, combine the butter, parsley, shallots, garlic powder, basil, salt, and the almonds, making a smooth paste.

Add the shrimp to a kettle of boiling water, along with the pickling spices, and cook for 3 minutes, or just until the shrimp turn pink.

Remove the kettle from the heat, and drain well.

Fill 12 of the hollowed-out halves with the cooked shrimp; divide the seasoned butter evenly among the rolls, and spoon it on top of the shrimp.

Top each roll with some of the reserved bread crumbs, and sprinkle with the white wine.

Place the filled rolls on a lightly greased baking sheet, and bake for 15 minutes.

Cover each roll with the remaining 12 halves, and bake for 10 minutes longer.

Serves 6 as a main dish, 12 as an appetizer.

MONTEREY BAY PRAWNS

This incredibly rich dish is from the famous Sardine Factory Restaurant in Monterey Bay, California. Needless to say, it should be reserved for a very special occasion.

---

2 pounds Monterey Bay prawns or large shrimp
Salt and freshly ground pepper
1 teaspoon paprika
½ cup olive oil
15 garlic cloves, finely chopped
8 shallots, minced
1 cup dry white wine
1 cup white wine vinegar
1 cup whipping cream
1 pound butter or margarine, cubed
6 tablespoons chopped fresh parsley

Preheat the oven to 500°F.

Split the prawns or shrimp, still in their shells, down the back; sprinkle them with salt and pepper to taste, and with the paprika.

Rub a baking sheet with enough olive oil to cover the sheet with a thin film; sprinkle 1 teaspoon of the chopped garlic on top.

Place the prawns on the baking sheet, and bake them for 3 to 4 minutes; remove them from the oven, and keep them warm while preparing the sauce.

Heat the remaining olive oil in a large skillet; add the remaining garlic and the shallots, and saute them for 2 minutes.

Add the wine and the vinegar, and bring to a boil; continue boiling until the liquid is nearly evaporated.

Add the cream, and cook over medium heat until the sauce is reduced by about one-half to a thick consistency.

Remove the sauce from the heat, and with a wire whisk, stir in the butter cube by cube. If the sauce gets too cold, heat it slightly, but be careful not to let it boil, or it will liquefy. The sauce should be just warm.

Season the sauce with salt and pepper to taste, and pour it over the prawns; garnish with the parsley before serving.

Serves 6 to 8.

CRAB ROLLS

---

1 pound crabmeat, drained and flaked
1 package (8 ounces) cream cheese, softened
1 teaspoon minced onion
1 teaspoon white horseradish
½ teaspoon curry powder
2 teaspoons lemon juice
2 teaspoons prepared mustard
Pinch of salt
½ cup mayonnaise
¼ cup dry white wine
6 French bread rolls
⅓ cup sliced blanched almonds
¼ cup grated Swiss or Gruyère cheese

Preheat the oven to 325°F.

In a medium bowl, combine the crabmeat with the cream cheese, onion, horseradish, curry powder, lemon juice, mustard, salt, mayonnaise, and the wine.

With a sharp knife, remove the top third from the rolls; hollow out the rolls, and set the "lids" aside.

Place the rolls in a large, shallow baking dish, and spoon the crab mixture evenly into them; sprinkle with the almonds and the cheese.

Bake the rolls for 20 minutes; replace the tops, and bake for another 5 minutes.

Serves 6.

COQUILLES ST. JACQUES MONTE CRISTO

A divine specialty I learned from my favorite French cooking instructor, Mrs. George Boxall.

1½ pounds sea scallops, washed and dried
½ teaspoon Hungarian paprika
1 lemon
½–¾ cup dry Madeira
6 tablespoons olive oil
6 tablespoons butter
1 tablespoon capers, drained
1 tablespoon fines herbes
Salt and pepper to taste

Place the scallops in a glass bowl, and sprinkle with the paprika and the juice of one-half of the lemon.

Pour the Madeira and 3 tablespoons of the olive oil over the scallops, and let them marinate at room temperature for several hours.

Drain the scallops well, and dry them on paper towels.

In a large skillet, heat the remaining olive oil with 3 tablespoons of the butter over medium-high heat.

When the oil and butter are hot, but not smoking, add the scallops, and sauté them quickly until lightly browned on both sides—about 4 to 5 minutes. Be careful not to overcook them, as that will toughen the scallops.

When the scallops are almost cooked, heat the remaining butter in a small, heavy saucepan over high heat so that it turns nut brown (*beurre noisette*).

The instant the butter has turned brown, add the juice from the other half of the lemon and the drained capers; remove the saucepan from the heat.

Remove the skillet from the heat, and season the scallops with the fines herbes and salt and pepper to taste.

Pour the butter-lemon mixture over the scallops, and serve them with boiled white rice, but no vegetables.

Serves 2 to 3.

SALMON AVOCADO BOATS

---

2 cans (7¾ ounces each) red salmon
2 ripe avocados
2 teaspoons lemon juice
½ cup mayonnaise
½ teaspoon dill weed
½ teaspoon garlic salt
2 teaspoons toasted sesame seeds

Drain the salmon, removing the skin and bones.

Cut the avocados in half, and remove the seeds. Place the halves in a serving dish, and sprinkle with the lemon juice.

In a small bowl, combine the mayonnaise, dill weed, garlic salt, and the sesame seeds.

Fold in the salmon, and spoon the mixture into the avocado halves.

If not serving right away, keep the dish refrigerated.

Serves 2 to 4.

Meatless

AVOCADO AND ARTICHOKE HEART QUICHE

1 ripe avocado, peeled and cut into slices
3 tablespoons lemon juice
3 eggs
1 cup whipping cream
¼ teaspoon cayenne pepper
Salt and freshly ground pepper to taste
8 canned artichoke hearts, cut into quarters
1 9-inch baked pie shell
½ cup grated Swiss or Gruyère cheese

Preheat the oven to 375°F.

Sprinkle the avocado slices with the lemon juice, and set aside.

In a medium bowl, beat the eggs; add the whipping cream, the cayenne, and salt and pepper to taste.

Stir in the avocado slices along with the quartered artichoke hearts.

Pour the mixture into the baked pie shell, and sprinkle the grated cheese on top.

Bake for 30 to 35 minutes, or until the filling is lightly browned on top, and a knife inserted in the center comes out clean.

Let the quiche cool on a wire rack for 5 minutes before slicing into wedges.

Serves 4 to 6.

QUESADILLAS FANG WITH SALSA PEDERSON

Pronounced kay-sah-dee-yahs, these are a real south-of-the-border treat. They make a perfect entree or appetizer for those who don't like spicy Mexican dishes.

---

12 7-inch flour tortillas
1 can (7 ounces) chopped green chilis, drained
¾ pound cheddar cheese, grated
¾ pound Monterey Jack cheese, grated
1 to 1½ cups unsalted butter (no substitutes)

Quickly wet each side of each tortilla with cold water. Lay the tortillas flat, side by side, on your work surface.

Place equal amounts of the chilis and the 2 cheeses on one half of each tortilla.

Fold the tortilla in half, and press the moist edges together to seal them shut. (If they should break or tear, don't worry about it!)

The tortillas may be frozen at this point if you are not ready to proceed.

In a large skillet, over high heat, melt 1 cup of butter until it is very hot.

Place a few of the quesadillas in the skillet, and sauté them until they are golden-brown; turn and sauté them on the other side.

Drain the quesadillas on paper towels as you remove them from the skillet. Keep them warm in a slow (200°F) oven until you are ready to serve them.

Continue cooking the remaining quesadillas, using more butter as needed.

Serve with or without Salsa Pederson (recipe follows).

Serves 6.

Note: As an appetizer, the quesadillas may be cut into small wedges.

SALSA PEDERSON

Similar to Hollandaise, this sauce also complements such cooked vegetables as asparagus, carrots, cauliflower, or broccoli.

---

7 tablespoons butter or margarine
1 onion, finely chopped
½ cup flour
Freshly ground nutmeg
2½ cups fresh or canned chicken broth
Salt and freshly ground pepper
3 egg yolks, slightly beaten
2 tablespoons lemon juice

Melt 4 tablespoons of the butter in a medium skillet, and sauté the onion until it is soft, about 3 minutes.

Stir in the flour, nutmeg, chicken broth, and salt and pepper to taste.

Cook, stirring, over medium heat until the mixture thickens and is smooth, about 8 to 10 minutes.

Remove the pan from the heat, and let the sauce cool.

Return the pan to low heat, and beat in the egg yolks, the remaining butter, and the lemon juice.

Cook the sauce, stirring constantly, for another 2 to 3 minutes.

Remove the pan from the heat, and stir for another minute or two.

Place the sauce in a refrigerator dish, cover it, and chill it before serving with the quesadillas. (For vegetables, the sauce may be served hot.)

The sauce will keep for several days in the refrigerator.

Makes about 3½ cups.

SPINACH ROULADE

A dazzling meatless main dish for a luncheon or a light supper.

SPINACH ROULADE:

3 tablespoons butter or margarine
1 package (10 ounces) frozen chopped spinach, defrosted
Salt and pepper to taste
5 eggs, separated
Freshly grated nutmeg
⅛ teaspoon cream of tartar

FILLING:

2 cups fresh mushrooms, sliced
1 tablespoon minced shallots
2 tablespoons butter or margarine
1 tablespoon lemon juice

SAUCE MORNAY:

5 tablespoons unsalted butter
¾ cup sifted flour
1 quart milk, scalded
Pinch of white pepper
Freshly grated nutmeg
1 teaspoon salt
¾ cup grated Swiss or Gruyère cheese
¾ cup grated Parmesan cheese
¼ cup whipping cream, as needed

Prepare the roulade: Melt the butter in a medium skillet, and cook the spinach until all the liquid has evaporated.

Season the spinach with salt and pepper to taste, and remove it from the heat; let the spinach cool to room temperature.

Preheat the oven to 400°F.

Add the egg yolks to the spinach, one at a time, mixing well; add some nutmeg to taste.

In a large bowl, with electric mixer at high speed, beat the egg whites with the cream of tartar until soft peaks form.

Fold the egg whites into the spinach mixture, and spread on a 10 × 15-inch jelly-roll pan that has been covered with parchment or waxed paper (lightly grease the paper).

Bake the spinach roulade for 10 minutes; remove the pan from the oven, and turn it out onto a lightly dampened dish towel; peel off the parchment or waxed paper, and discard it.

While the roulade is baking, cook the mushrooms in the butter in a medium skillet until tender; add the shallots, and cook 2 minutes longer.

Stir in the lemon juice, remove the skillet from the heat, and set aside.

Prepare the sauce Mornay: Melt the butter in a large saucepan over medium-high heat.

With a wire whisk, stir in the flour; reduce the heat, and cook the mixture for 10 minutes.

Add the scalded milk, and beat with a wire whisk until the sauce is smooth.

Stir in the seasonings, the Swiss cheese, and one-half of the Parmesan cheese; if the sauce is too thick, stir in a little whipping cream. Continue cooking the sauce until the cheeses are melted.

Mix the mushrooms with 1 cup of the sauce, and spread this mixture evenly over the roulade.

Start rolling up the roulade lengthwise, using the dish towel to help you roll; place the roulade on a large, shallow baking dish.

Spoon about 1 cup of the sauce over the roulade, and sprinkle it with the remaining Parmesan cheese.

If desired, roulade can be returned quickly to the oven, or put under the broiler just long enough to heat it through. If the sauce and the filling are still quite warm, this is not necessary.

To serve, cut the roulade horizontally into slices, and pass the remaining sauce separately.

Serves 6 to 8.

CHEESE–SPINACH SOUFFLÉ

---

6 tablespoons butter or margarine
6 tablespoons flour
1 cup milk
Salt and pepper to taste
¼ teaspoon dry mustard
Pinch of nutmeg
1½ cups grated cheddar cheese
1 package (10 ounces) frozen chopped spinach, cooked
  and well drained
6 eggs, separated
¼ teaspoon cream of tartar

Melt the butter in a medium saucepan, and with a wire whisk, beat in the flour, stirring until smooth.

Gradually stir in the milk, and cook over medium heat until the mixture is thick.

Add the seasonings and the cheese, and continue cooking until the cheese has melted.

Stir in the cooked spinach, and remove the saucepan from the heat. Pour the mixture into a large bowl, and let it cool.

Preheat the oven to 350°F.

In a medium bowl, with electric mixer at medium speed, beat the egg yolks until thick and lemon-colored—about 5 minutes.

Stir a little of the cheese sauce into the egg yolks, and then pour the yolks back into the cheese sauce, mixing well.

Thoroughly wash and dry the beaters, and in a large bowl, with the electric mixer at high speed, beat the egg whites with the cream of tartar until stiff peaks form.

With a rubber scraper, gently fold the whites into the cheese mixture, making sure that no clumps of egg white remain.

Transfer the mixture to a well greased 2-quart soufflé dish (with straight sides), and bake for 45 minutes, or until the soufflé is puffy and golden brown. Serve immediately.

Serves 4.

OMELETTE PIPERADE

A favorite recipe, with a southern French accent, from a very dear cooking "buddy."

---

2 to 3 tablespoons corn oil
1 onion, thinly sliced
1 green pepper, thinly sliced
2 tomatoes, peeled
1 garlic clove, minced
4 eggs
⅛ teaspoon salt
Pinch of freshly ground pepper
¼ cup minced parsley
1 tablespoon butter

Heat 2 tablespoons of the oil in a small skillet, and add the onions and the green pepper; cook over low heat until the onion is soft.

Cover the skillet, and continue cooking the vegetables over low heat until they are very tender—5 to 7 minutes.

Meanwhile, seed the tomatoes, and let the juice drain out. Then dice them into ½-inch cubes.

Heat a little bit of oil in another small skillet, and add the tomatoes. Do not let them get mushy; just cook them enough to allow the juice to evaporate.

Add the garlic to the tomatoes, and cook for another minute.

Place the tomato mixture and the onions and peppers in a colander, and let them stand for a few minutes.

Make the omelette at the last minute: Beat the eggs with the salt and pepper, and add the parsley.

Preheat the oven to 400°F.

Melt the butter in a 10-inch omelette pan with a heatproof handle.

As soon as the butter is foaming and *almost* turning color, add the egg mixture, and cook over medium-high heat until the eggs are set on the bottom.

Spread the vegetable mixture evenly over the eggs, and place the omelette pan in the oven for about 2 minutes, or until the top is puffed and brown. Watch it carefully, as it takes only a short time to cook on top.

Serves 2 to 3.

HINT

In the making of omelettes, the butter should be hot enough to form a film that insulates the egg mixture from the bottom of the pan. If the butter is only warm, it will mix with the eggs, yielding an omelette that sticks to the pan and has the consistency of scrambled eggs.

BAKED ZITI CASSEROLE

This distant cousin of lasagne is so satisfying that no one will notice that the meat is missing from the sauce! You can, in fact, use this sauce with any variety of pasta dishes.

MEATLESS MARINARA:

¼ cup olive oil
2 garlic cloves, crushed
1 large onion, chopped
¼ pound fresh mushrooms, sliced
1 green pepper, cut in thin strips (optional)
1 can (28 ounces) concentrated crushed tomatoes
1 can (8 ounces) tomato sauce
1 can (6 ounces) tomato paste
2 teaspoons oregano
1 teaspoon basil
1 teaspoon garlic salt
1 teaspoon sugar
Pinch of cinnamon
1 pound ziti macaroni

FILLING:

2 cups cottage cheese, drained
½ pound mozzarella cheese, cubed
⅔ cup grated Parmesan cheese
2 eggs, slightly beaten
1 tablespoon minced parsley
1 teaspoon salt
¼ teaspoon freshly ground pepper

To prepare the sauce, heat the olive oil in a large skillet over medium heat, and add the garlic, onion, mushrooms, and the optional green pepper; cook until the vegetables are tender but not brown.

Add the concentrated tomatoes, tomato sauce, tomato paste, and the seasonings.

Reduce the heat, cover the skillet, and cook for 1 hour, stirring occasionally.

Meanwhile, cook the ziti according to the package directions; rinse in cold water, and drain well.

In a medium bowl, combine the cottage cheese, mozzarella, 1/3 cup of the Parmesan cheese, the eggs, parsley, salt and pepper.

Preheat the oven to 350° F.

Spoon a small amount of the marinara sauce into the bottom of a 5-quart casserole.

Top with one half of the ziti, then one half of the cheese filling, and one half of the remaining marinara; sprinkle with a little of the remaining Parmesan.

Repeat the layers with the remaining ziti, cheese filling, and sauce; sprinkle with the remaining Parmesan.

Bake, uncovered, for 45 minutes, or until the sauce is bubbly.

Serves 10 to 12.

CHAPTER 3

ACCOMPANIMENTS

Rice & Noodles
Potatoes & Vegetables
Salads & Fruits

Rice & Noodles

LAUREL RICE

The laurel, or bay leaf, imparts a subtle, delicate flavor to this dish.

---

2 tablespoons butter or margarine
1 small onion, chopped
1 clove garlic, minced
1 cup long grain white rice, uncooked
1 bay leaf
2¼ cups fresh or canned chicken broth

Melt the butter in a medium saucepan, and sauté the onion and garlic until tender but not brown.

Add the rice and the bay leaf, and cook, stirring constantly, for 2 minutes.

Meanwhile, heat the chicken broth in a small saucepan just to the boiling point.

Add the broth to the rice mixture, lower the heat, and simmer, covered, for exactly 20 minutes.

Remove the bay leaf, and discard it. The rice will stay hot for up to 30 minutes if left covered.

Serves 4.

The secret of cooking perfect rice is to simmer the ingredients over low heat without stirring or removing the pot lid during the cooking time. This allows the steam to circulate properly.

There are three basic types of rice. The short grain variety is characterized by grains that are about twice as long as they are wide; when cooked, this rice is moist and tender. It is ideal for puddings, stuffings, and Oriental cooking. Long grain rice, when cooked, yields a firm, dry product; the grains do not stick together. Milled rice has the hull and most of the bran layers removed. It does not have to be washed.

CONFETTI RICE

1 cup long grain white rice, uncooked
1 package (10 ounces) frozen peas
5 tablespoons butter or margarine
1 cup sliced fresh mushrooms
1 small onion, finely chopped
1 teaspoon salt
¼ teaspoon freshly ground pepper
¼ teaspoon rosemary leaves, crumbled
¼ cup slivered almonds, blanched and toasted

Cook the rice according to the package directions.

Cook the peas according to the package directions, just until heated through but still firm. Drain well, and set aside.

Melt the butter in a large skillet over medium heat, and sauté the mushrooms and onion until the onion is transparent but not brown.

Add the rice, the peas, and the seasonings, stirring well.

Stir in the almonds, tossing to blend in with the other ingredients.

Serves 6.

HINT

To blanch almonds, place shelled almonds in boiling water for 1 minute; drain. When the almonds are cool enough to handle, the outer skins will slide right off. Cut them into slivers with a sharp knife. Almonds may be toasted by placing them on a cookie sheet in a slow oven for 15 minutes.

LEMON RICE

The combination of lemon and rice is both unique and delicious. It will go with almost any chicken recipe.

2½ cups fresh or canned chicken broth
1 tablespoon lemon juice
1½ teaspoons salt
1 bay leaf
¼ teaspoon white pepper
½ cup butter
1 cup long grain white rice, uncooked

In the top part of a double boiler, over direct heat, cook the chicken stock, lemon juice, salt, bay leaf, pepper, and one-half of the butter until hot.

Stir in the rice.

Place the mixture over the bottom part of a double boiler, which should be filled with gently boiling water.

Cover the top part, and cook for 35 minutes, stirring occasionally.

Remove from the heat; remove the bay leaf, and discard it.

Just before serving, toss the rice with the remaining butter.

Serves 4.

MUSHROOM–NOODLE CASSEROLE

This is one of many noodle puddings, and it's filling enough to serve as a main dish. It's also an excellent accompaniment to pot roast.

---

1 package (8 ounces) broad noodles
3 tablespoons butter or margarine
1 small onion, finely chopped
¼ pound mushrooms, sliced
8 ounces cream cheese, softened
1 cup sour cream
1 can (10¾ ounces) cream of mushroom soup
½ soup can milk
½ teaspoon Worcestershire sauce
½ teaspoon salt
½ teaspoon garlic salt
Dash of curry powder
Dash of Tabasco sauce
½ cup unseasoned bread crumbs

Cook the noodles according to the package directions; drain well.

Preheat the oven to 350°F. Grease a 2-quart casserole.

Melt 2 tablespoons of the butter in a small skillet, and sauté the onion and mushrooms until soft but not brown; set aside.

In a large bowl, with the electric mixer at low speed, combine the cream cheese, sour cream, mushroom soup, milk, and the seasonings.

Add the noodles to the cream cheese mixture, stirring well with a wooden spoon.

Add the onions and the mushrooms.

Pour the mixture into the prepared casserole, and sprinkle the bread crumbs on top; dot with the remaining butter.

Bake, uncovered, for 30 minutes.

Serves 6 as a main dish, 12 as a side dish.

NOODLE KUGEL I

A kugel is a puddinglike cake (or maybe it's a cake-like pudding) that figures prominently in Jewish cooking. Although these combinations are not kosher, the kugel below goes beautifully with meat loaf, poultry, and ham.

---

1 pound medium or broad noodles
½ cup raisins or dried apricots, cut in small pieces
   (optional)
1 pint (2 cups) sour cream
½ cup sugar, or to taste
8 ounces cream cheese, softened
3 eggs
1 tablespoon vanilla
½ cup cornflake crumbs or graham cracker crumbs

Cook the noodles according to the package directions; drain well.

Preheat the oven to 350°F. Grease 9 × 13-inch baking dish.

If using raisins or apricots, cover them with hot water, and let them stand while preparing the remainder of the recipe.

In a large bowl, with the electric mixer at low speed, combine the sour cream, sugar, cream cheese, eggs, and the vanilla, until smooth.

Stir in the noodles, mixing well.

Drain the water from the fruit, and add the fruit to the noodle mixture.

Turn the mixture into the prepared baking dish, and sprinkle with the cornflakes or graham cracker crumbs.

Bake for 30 to 40 minutes, or until a knife inserted in the center comes out clean.

Cut into squares, and serve hot or at room temperature.

Serves 12 to 15.

NOODLE KUGEL II

This recipe is for those who prefer a less sweet noodle pudding.

8 ounces medium or broad noodles
1 cup sour cream
2 tablespoons lemon juice
1 tablespoon Worcestershire sauce
½ pound Swiss cheese, grated
½ cup unseasoned bread crumbs
2 tablespoons butter or margarine

Cook the noodles according to the package directions; drain well.

Meanwhile, preheat the oven to 350°F. Grease a 2-quart casserole.

In a large bowl, combine the noodles with the sour cream, lemon juice, Worcestershire sauce, and the Swiss cheese, mixing well.

Turn the mixture into the prepared casserole, and sprinkle the bread crumbs on top; dot with the butter.

Bake for 45 to 55 minutes, or until the top is nicely brown.

Serve hot or at room temperature.

Serves 6.

Potatoes & Vegetables

POTATO PIE

---

1 pound cottage cheese, well drained
2 cups mashed potatoes
½ cup sour cream
2 eggs
Pinch of salt
⅛ teaspoon cayenne pepper
½ cup thinly sliced scallions
10-inch unbaked pie shell
5 tablespoons grated Parmesan cheese

Preheat the oven to 450°F.

In a large bowl, with the electric mixer at medium speed, beat the cottage cheese until it is smooth.

Add the mashed potatoes, and continue to beat well.

Add the sour cream, eggs, and the seasonings, beating until smooth.

Stir in the scallions.

Pour the mixture into the unbaked pie shell, and sprinkle the top with the grated cheese.

Bake for 50 minutes, or until the top is golden brown.

Let the pie cool on a wire rack 10 minutes before serving.

Serves 6 to 8.

POTATOES OUTRAGEOUS

3 tablespoons butter or margarine
1 small onion, chopped
4 cups mashed potatoes (made from instant potatoes or
    from scratch)
Salt and pepper to taste
1 package (11 ounces) buttermilk biscuit mix
Oil for deep frying

Melt the butter in a small skillet, and sauté the onion until soft and golden—about 2 minutes.

Add the onion to the mashed potatoes, mixing well; season with salt and pepper to taste.

Prepare the biscuit mix according to the package directions.

With a round cookie or biscuit cutter, cut out 3-inch circles from the dough.

Place a few tablespoons of the potato mixture in the center of each biscuit; fold the biscuit in half, crimping the edges to seal it well.

In a deep fat fryer or a skillet with a thermometer, heat about 2 cups of oil to 375°F.

Fry the filled biscuits until they are golden brown and puffed up; drain on paper towels, and serve hot.

The fried puffs can also be frozen after they have cooled. To reheat them, place them on a cookie sheet directly from the freezer, and bake in a preheated 400°F oven for about 10 minutes.

Serves 10.

POTATO SKINS

I discovered this delightful treat on a recent trip to Los Angeles, and now it's finding its way onto many restaurant menus.

---

6 whole baking potatoes, scrubbed and washed
2 cups grated cheddar cheese
½ pound bacon, cooked, drained, and crumbled
(optional)

Preheat the oven to 375°F.

Bake the potatoes for 1 hour, or until they are tender but still firm.

Remove the potatoes from the oven. Turn the oven heat up to Broil.

Cut the potatoes in half lengthwise, and scoop out the pulp, leaving about ¼ inch of potato in the bottom of each skin. (Use the pulp to make mashed potatoes.)

Cover the bottom of each potato shell with the cheese and the optional bacon.

Place the filled skins on a lightly greased baking sheet, and broil them just until the cheese begins to burn slightly; watch them carefully.

Serve immediately, garnished with sour cream and chives, if desired.

Serves 6.

Note: For those who prefer potato skins plain, follow instructions above, except omit the cheese and bacon; brush inside of potato skin lightly with melted butter and a little salt before broiling until lightly browned and crisp. Watch carefully and serve hot.

SWEET POTATO–PINEAPPLE CASSEROLE

The marriage of sweet potatoes and pineapple was made in heaven. This casserole, which is not overly sweet, goes nicely with a holiday ham or turkey.

---

4 cups cooked mashed sweet potatoes (about 2½ pounds
    of fresh sweet potatoes, boiled, or 2 22-ounce cans of
    sweet potatoes or yams)
6 tablespoons melted butter or margarine
¾ cup orange juice
1 can (15 ounces) crushed pineapple, drained
1 teaspoon salt
¼ teaspoon paprika
1 cup shredded coconut

Preheat the oven to 400°F.

Place the sweet potatoes in a large bowl, and add the butter, beating with a wooden spoon or an electric mixer.

Beat in the orange juice, pineapple, and salt.

Spoon the mixture into a greased 2-quart casserole, and sprinkle the top with the paprika.

Bake, covered with foil, for 30 minutes; remove the casserole from the oven, and set the oven to Broil.

Sprinkle the coconut evenly over the sweet potatoes, and broil the casserole for 3 minutes, or until the coconut is nicely toasted. Watch the casserole carefully, as the coconut can burn easily.

Serves 8 to 10.

FLUFFY CORN FRITTERS

---

1 can (12 ounces) corn, well drained, or 2 cups fresh
   corn, cooked
½ cup milk
2 cups flour
1 teaspoon salt
¼ teaspoon freshly ground pepper
1 tablespoon baking powder
1 tablespoon salad oil
2 eggs, well beaten
Additional oil for deep frying

In a medium bowl, combine the corn with the milk.

Sift together the flour, salt, pepper, and the baking powder, and add to the corn mixture.

Add the oil and the beaten eggs.

In a deep fryer, heat oil as recommended by manufacturer to 375°F. (If you do not have a deep fryer, use a large skillet and a deep-fat thermometer.)

Drop the batter by tablespoonfuls into the hot oil, and cook, turning once, until fritters are golden brown.

Remove the fritters as they brown, and let them drain on paper towels.

Serve hot with applesauce or maple syrup.

Makes about 2 dozen.

VEGETABLE SOUFFLÉ

This recipe just might turn the most determined vegetable hater into a vegetable lover.

---

2 packages (10 ounces each) Stouffer's frozen spinach soufflé
2 packages (10 ounces each) Stouffer's frozen corn soufflé
2 packages (10 ounces each) frozen glazed carrots

Preheat the oven to 350°F. Grease a large, shallow baking dish.

Remove the frozen spinach and corn soufflés from their packages, and place them side by side in the prepared baking dish.

Sprinkle the glazed carrots over the soufflés.

Cover the baking dish, and bake the mixture for 1½ hours.

Just before serving, stir thoroughly.

Serves 8–12.

VEGETABLE NESTS

An interesting combination of textures and flavors for vegetable fanciers of all ages.

---

1 package frozen patty shells
½ pound mushrooms, sliced
2 tablespoons butter or margarine
½ teaspoon garlic powder
1½ cups broccoli flowerettes (fresh or frozen)
2 small zucchini, cubed
2 large carrots, peeled and cut into thin strips
½ cup sliced red bell pepper
½ cup sliced green bell pepper
½ teaspoon marjoram, crushed
1½ cups chicken broth
Salt and freshly ground pepper to taste
2 tablespoons cornstarch
¼ cup water

Preheat the oven to 425°F.

Bake the patty shells according to the package directions. When cool enough to handle, remove the doughy centers, leaving only the bottom and sides as a shell.

In a large skillet, sauté the mushrooms in the butter with the garlic powder over medium heat.

Add the remaining vegetables, the marjoram, and the chicken broth, and bring to a boil.

Reduce the heat, cover the skillet, and simmer for about 10 minutes, or until the vegetables are tender.

Add the salt and pepper to taste.

Blend the cornstarch with the water, and add the mixture to the skillet.

Cook, stirring constantly, until the mixture is thickened and smooth.

Spoon the mixture into the prepared patty shells, and serve hot.

Serves 6.

HINTS

When you cook fresh vegetables, they'll retain their maximum wholesomeness if you reduce the amount of water used and reduce the cooking time.

For many recipes, such as the one above, a certain amount of cutting, paring, and shredding is necessary; but when serving plain fresh vegetables, you should limit the amount of exposed surfaces by doing less cutting. This insures that the vitamin content will be retained.

STIR–FRY FRESH VEGETABLES

The beauty of this recipe is that you can use any combination of fresh vegetables, enabling you to take advantage of whatever specials your local market is offering.

---

2 to 3 tablespoons corn oil
2 cloves garlic, crushed
¼ teaspoon grated fresh ginger, or ½ teaspoon powdered ginger
1 cup beef or chicken stock
1 beef or chicken bouillon cube
¼ cup soy sauce
¼ cup cornstarch
Any of the following fresh vegetables (about 8 cups in all):
Carrots, cut in 2-inch strips
Cauliflower, in flowerettes
Broccoli, in flowerettes
Mushrooms, cut in quarters
Celery, sliced thickly on the diagonal
Chinese cabbage (bok choy), thinly sliced
Cabbage, cut into 1-inch squares
Fresh bean sprouts
Onions, coarsely chopped
Green pepper, cut into strips or squares
Water chestnuts (canned), well drained and sliced

In a wok, over medium heat, heat the oil, and add the garlic and ginger. Let cook for 2 minutes.

Meanwhile, heat the broth in a small saucepan, and dissolve the bouillon cube in it.

Remove from the heat, and stir in the soy sauce and cornstarch, mixing well.

Add the sauce to the wok, stirring constantly; the sauce will become thick and translucent quite rapidly.

Then add the chosen vegetables in sequence based on the

length of cooking time required by each vegetable. The firmer vegetables (carrots, broccoli) should come first, followed by medium-firm varieties (green pepper, celery, cabbage, onions), and finally the softest ones (mushrooms, bean sprouts). Total cooking time should be about 7 minutes, as vegetables should all be crisp.

Serves 6 to 8.

EGGPLANT MELANGE

---

1 medium (about 2 pounds) eggplant
6 tablespoons olive oil
1 pound small mushrooms, cleaned and trimmed
1 garlic clove, minced
1 teaspoon oregano
Salt and pepper to taste
1 cup fresh or frozen green peas, cooked
1 can (16 ounces) Italian plum tomatoes

Peel the eggplant, and cut it in half lengthwise; cut the halves into slices about ¼ inch thick.

Heat 4 tablespoons of the olive oil in a large skillet, and sauté the eggplant slices until they are golden; remove the slices and drain them on paper towels.

Heat the remaining oil in the same skillet, and sauté the mushrooms and garlic for 1 to 2 minutes.

Add the oregano, salt, and pepper, and sauté the mixture for about 10 minutes over medium heat; mushrooms should be tender but still firm.

Stir in the peas, the reserved eggplant, and the tomatoes. Crush the tomatoes as you stir them into the skillet.

Simmer the mixture for 15 minutes; taste and correct the seasonings.

Serves 6.

RATATOUILLE NIÇOISE

¼ cup olive oil
5 or 6 cloves garlic, crushed
1 medium onion, chopped
1 green pepper, seeded and cut into thin strips
1 small eggplant, unpeeled, cut into cubes
2 medium zucchini, cubed
¼ cup flour
2 or 3 large tomatoes
Salt and freshly ground pepper to taste
1 can (6 ounces) tomato paste

In a large kettle, heat the olive oil over medium-high heat.

Add the garlic, onion, and green pepper, and sauté the mixture until the vegetables are tender but not brown.

In a large bowl, toss the eggplant and zucchini with the flour, and add this mixture to the kettle.

Cover the kettle, and cook over low heat for 1 hour, stirring occasionally.

Meanwhile, peel the tomatoes by plunging them in boiling water for 30 seconds. Remove the tomatoes with a fork, and the skins should slide right off. Pare away the stem ends, and coarsely chop the tomatoes.

Place the chopped tomatoes in a colander to drain off the excess liquid.

After 1 hour has elapsed, add the tomatoes to the kettle, along with salt and pepper to taste and the tomato paste.

Cook, uncovered, for 15 minutes. The mixture should be very thick.

The Ratatouille may be served hot, at room temperature, or chilled.

Serves 6 to 8.

TANGY ZUCCHINI

4 medium zucchini
⅔ cup mayonnaise
2 tablespoons crumbled bleu cheese
¼ cup grated Parmesan cheese
¼ teaspoon garlic powder

Preheat the oven to Broil.

Place the whole zucchini in a large kettle of boiling water, and parboil them for 5 minutes.

Drain the zucchini well, and cut them in half lengthwise.

Place the zucchini halves on a lightly greased broiler pan.

In a small bowl, combine the mayonnaise with the cheeses and the garlic powder. Spread this mixture evenly over the zucchini halves.

Broil the zucchini just until the topping is golden brown and bubbly, about 3 minutes.

Serves 4.

SPICED ACORN SQUASH

This is the perfect accompaniment to roast pork or ham.

---

4 acorn squash
½ cup dark brown sugar
1½ teaspoons cinnamon
¼ teaspoon nutmeg
¼ teaspoon ground cloves
Pinch of salt
½ cup melted butter or margarine
½ cup maple syrup
2 cups (approximately) boiling water

Preheat the oven to 350°F.

Cut each squash in half lengthwise, and scoop out the seeds and fibers.

In a small bowl combine the sugar, spices, salt, and the butter.

Arrange the squash halves in a large shallow baking dish, and spoon the butter mixture evenly into the eight halves.

Pour 1 tablespoon of the maple syrup into each half.

Pour the boiling water into the bottom of the baking dish around the squash halves, being careful not to get water near the tops.

Bake uncovered for 30 minutes. Serve hot.

Serves 8.

JACK–O'–LANTERN COMPOTE

A colorful side dish to serve with almost any autumn menu.

1 small pumpkin
2 or 3 large tart apples, peeled and chopped (about 2
   cups)
1 cup yellow raisins
¾ cup chopped pecans
⅓ cup water
⅓ cup sugar
1 teaspoon lemon juice
1 teaspoon grated lemon peel
¼ teaspoon cinnamon
Freshly grated nutmeg to taste

Preheat the oven to 350°F.

Wash and dry the pumpkin. Cut off the top, leaving a nice slice for the lid.

Place the pumpkin in a large shallow baking dish, and scoop out all the seeds. (These may be baked separately for a nutritious snack.)

Combine the remaining ingredients in a medium saucepan, and bring to a boil.

Pour the apple mixture into the pumpkin, and cover it with the lid.

Bake for 45 to 55 minutes, or until the apples are tender.

When serving, be sure to scoop out some of the pumpkin meat. This compote can be served hot or at room temperature.

Serves 6 to 8.

> **HINT**
>
> Heat and air can cause raisins to dry out, and humidity will cause the sugar in the fruit to crystallize. Therefore, raisins should be stored in the refrigerator in an airtight container or plastic bag.

CARROT PÂTÉ

An interesting way to serve an otherwise unexciting vegetable.

---

3 jars (1 pound each) sliced carrots, well drained
3 large eggs
1 package (10 ounces) frozen chopped spinach, thawed
   and well drained
½ teaspoon salt
Freshly ground nutmeg to taste
Freshly ground pepper to taste

Preheat the oven to 375°F.

In a blender or food processor, puree the carrots.

Add 2 of the eggs, and blend or process until smooth. Remove the mixture from the container, and set aside.

Combine the spinach with the remaining egg, and ¼ teaspoon of the salt, as well as nutmeg and pepper to taste.

Combine the remaining seasonings with the carrot mixture.

Grease a 9 × 5-inch loaf pan, and line it with parchment or brown paper; grease the paper.

Place one-half of the carrot mixture in the pan; bang the pan against the counter to set the carrot mixture.

Spread all of the spinach mixture evenly over the carrot layer.

Cover the spinach with the remaining carrot mixture.

Cover the pan with a piece of greased parchment or aluminum foil.

Place the loaf pan in a shallow baking dish filled with about 1 to 1½ inches of boiling water.

Bake the pâté in the "water bath" for about 1½ hours. Turn off the oven heat, and let the pâté rest in the oven for 10 minutes.

Remove the loaf pan to a wire rack to cool for 30 minutes.

Unmold the pâté onto a serving platter, and serve warm or cold, cut into slices.

Serves 12.

SWEET & SOUR CARROTS

Even those who dislike cooked carrots should go for this recipe.

---

3 pounds carrots, peeled and cut into 1½-inch strips
1 can (10¾ ounces) tomato soup, undiluted
1 cup cider vinegar
1 cup sugar
1½ cups salad oil
1 teaspoon dry mustard
1 green pepper, finely chopped
1 medium onion, finely chopped

The day before serving, bring 4 quarts of salted water to a boil in a large kettle.

Add the carrots, and cook them until they are tender but not too soft.

Drain the carrots well.

In a large glass or plastic bowl, combine the remaining ingredients, mixing well.

Add the carrots, mixing until they are well coated with the marinade.

Cover the bowl and refrigerate the carrots overnight, longer if desired.

Serves 10 to 12.

FRIED BEER BATTER ASPARAGUS

This recipe is another favorite from Josephine's Restaurant.

1½ cups flour
1½ cups flat beer (let beer stand, uncapped, at room
    temperature for at least 1 hour)
Salt and freshly ground pepper to taste
1 tablespoon melted butter or margarine
1 egg
3 to 4 cups shortening or salad oil for deep frying
1½ pounds fresh asparagus, cleaned and with bottoms
    trimmed off

In a large bowl, combine the flour, beer, salt and pepper to taste, with the melted butter and the egg; beat well with a wire whisk to remove all lumps.

Cover the batter, and let it stand at room temperature for at least 30 minutes.

In an electric skillet or a deep fat fryer with a thermostat, heat the shortening or oil to 375°F.

Dip the asparagus spears in the batter, turning to coat them well.

Drop the spears into the hot shortening or oil, and fry them until they are golden brown, turning them with a pair of tongs.

Drain the spears well on paper towels, and serve them immediately.

Serves 4 to 6.

GNOCCHI VERDI

Flavorful and light, these are also known as spinach dumplings.

6 tablespoons butter or margarine
1 tablespoon finely chopped onion
3 packages (10 ounces each) frozen chopped spinach,
   thawed and drained
1 cup ricotta cheese or well-drained cottage cheese
¾ cup flour
1 cup grated Parmesan cheese
¾ teaspoon salt
½ teaspoon pepper
¼ teaspoon garlic powder
¼ teaspoon ground nutmeg
2 tablespoons chopped parsley
2 eggs, slightly beaten
Additional flour for coating gnocchi
12 cups water
3 tablespoons instant chicken bouillon (or 3 bouillon
   cubes)
¼ cup melted butter or margarine

Heat the 6 tablespoons of butter in a large skillet; add the onion, and cook until it is tender.

Add the spinach; cook, stirring, over medium heat until the spinach is quite dry, 4 to 5 minutes.

Mix in the ricotta or cottage cheese; cook for 3 minutes, and then transfer the mixture to a large bowl.

Add the flour, ½ cup of the Parmesan cheese, the salt, pepper, garlic powder, nutmeg, and the parsley.

Let the mixture cool for 5 minutes, and then stir in the eggs.

Drop the spinach mixture, 2 tablespoons at a time, into a small bowl of flour; gently roll the mixture to coat it with the flour, and shape it into balls about 1½ inches in diameter. Continue this procedure, placing the spinach balls on a large plate as you make them.

Place the water and chicken bouillon in a 4-quart kettle, and heat to a boil.

Reduce the heat and simmer, stirring to dissolve the bouillon.

Drop the spinach balls into the broth; cook them, uncovered, until the gnocchi are quite firm and rise to the top of the broth —about 10 minutes. (Avoid overcrowding; cook the gnocchi in several batches, if necessary.) As the gnocchi cook, remove with a slotted spoon, and place them in a large serving dish.

Drizzle the gnocchi with the ¼ cup of melted butter, and sprinkle with the remaining Parmesan cheese; serve at once with additional Parmesan, if desired.

Serves 8.

BROCCOLI WITH LEMON

1 bunch fresh broccoli
¼ cup olive oil
1 garlic clove, minced
2 tablespoons lemon juice

Remove the leaves from the broccoli, and cut off the tough portions of the stems.

Wash the broccoli thoroughly, drain it, and separate the larger stalks into quarters.

In a large kettle, bring 6 cups of salted water to a boil, and add the broccoli. Cook, covered, for 8 minutes, or until the broccoli is slightly tender but still has its brilliant green color.

Drain the broccoli well, and keep it warm.

In the same kettle, heat the olive oil and garlic until the oil is bubbly, but do not let the garlic brown.

Add the broccoli, sprinkle with the lemon juice, and cook, covered, for 1 minute, or until the broccoli is well heated. Serve hot.

Serves 4.

SOUR CREAM SAUCE FOR VEGETABLES

This sauce will enhance baked potatoes, asparagus, and other green vegetables. Use your imagination.

---

1 cup sour cream
1 teaspoon lemon juice
Freshly ground pepper to taste
¼ teaspoon salt
2 tablespoons prepared white horseradish, drained

Combine all the ingredients, and chill until ready to serve. Spoon the sauce over baked potatoes or another cooked vegetable.

Makes about 1¼ cups of sauce.

> **HINT**
>
> Another nice seasoning for potatoes and vegetables is a French standby known as *quatre épices,* a blend of 4 spices. It is also used to season white sauces and mild flavored soups, as well as meats and meat loaves. Usually ¼ teaspoon of the blend is enough. To prepare your own mixture, blend together ¼ cup white pepper, 1 tablespoon ground ginger, 1 tablespoon of nutmeg, and 1¼ tablespoons of ground cloves. Store the mixture in a jar with a tight-fitting lid, and use as desired.

Salads & Fruits

HEAVENLY SALAD

A most serviceable recipe when you're asked to "bring a dish" to a group dinner or community event.

1 package (6 ounces) lime gelatin
1 can (8 ounces) crushed pineapple, well drained
1 package (3 ounces) lemon pudding and pie-filling mix
1½ cups miniature marshmallows
3 or 4 bananas, sliced
2 cups whipped cream or prepared whipped topping

Prepare the lime gelatin according to the package directions, and stir in the crushed pineapple.

Pour the mixture into a 9 × 13-inch pan, and chill until set, about 2 hours.

Meanwhile, prepare the lemon pudding according to the package directions; set aside to cool.

When the gelatin is set, place the marshmallows and sliced bananas evenly across the top.

Fold the whipped cream or whipped topping into the cooled lemon pudding, and spread this mixture over the marshmallows and bananas.

Chill the salad for several hours before serving.

Serves 12 to 15.

FRUITED COLE SLAW

In winter, when lettuce is likely to be higher priced, cabbage is a nutritious, delicious substitute.

¼ cup light cream or evaporated milk
1 cup mayonnaise
1 small onion, finely chopped
½ teaspoon salt, or to taste
Freshly ground pepper to taste
1 medium head (about 2 pounds) cabbage, shredded
4 carrots, peeled and grated
1 can (20 ounces) crushed pineapple, drained
1 can (15 ounces) pineapple chunks, drained
2 apples, chopped (do not peel them)

In a small bowl, combine the cream, mayonnaise, onion, salt, and pepper. Place the mixture in the refrigerator for 30 minutes.

In a large bowl, toss together the cabbage, carrots, the two kinds of pineapple, and the apples.

Pour the dressing over the salad, tossing well.

Cover the bowl, and refrigerate the salad for several hours. This salad tastes best when served very cold.

Serves 8 to 10.

HINT

To prevent boiled cabbage from leaving a strong cooking odor in the kitchen, add 2 slices of white bread to the pot while it is boiling.

CABBAGE WALDORF SALAD

---

1 medium head (about 2 pounds) cabbage, shredded
2 or 3 stalks celery, finely chopped
2 apples, chopped (do not peel)
½ cup raisins
1 cup mayonnaise
¼ cup cider vinegar
2 tablespoons sugar, or to taste
½ cup coarsely chopped walnuts

In a large bowl, combine the cabbage with the celery, apples, and the raisins.

Add the mayonnaise, the vinegar and the sugar, mixing well. Taste the salad; if it seems too tart, add more sugar. If it's too bland, add a little more vinegar.

Stir in the walnuts.

Cover the salad, and refrigerate it until serving.

Serves 6 to 8.

ORANGE AVOCADO SALAD

1 medium head (about 1½ pounds) romaine lettuce
1 cucumber, peeled and sliced
1 ripe avocado, seeded, peeled, and sliced
1 can (11 ounces) mandarin orange sections, well drained
2 tablespoons sliced scallions

DRESSING:

2 teaspoons grated orange peel
¼ cup orange juice
½ cup salad oil
2 tablespoons sugar
2 tablespoons red wine vinegar
1 tablespoon lemon juice
Salt and freshly ground pepper to taste

Wash the lettuce leaves well; dry them thoroughly, and tear them into bite-size pieces.

In a large bowl, combine the lettuce with the cucumber, avocado, orange sections, and the scallions.

Make the dressing by combining all the ingredients in a blender container. Blend at high speed for 30 seconds. (If you do not have a blender, combine all the ingredients in a jar with a tight-fitting lid, and shake well.)

Pour the dressing over the salad just before serving, tossing well to coat all the salad ingredients.

Serves 6 to 8.

PEPPERONI SALAD

When the family gets bored with ordinary salad, surprise them with this creation.

---

1 medium onion, thinly sliced
1 stick (8 ounces) pepperoni, thinly sliced
¼ cup crumbled bleu cheese
⅔ cup salad oil
⅓ cup cider vinegar
Salt and freshly ground pepper to taste
1 bag (10 ounces) fresh spinach, washed, thoroughly
    dried, and chopped
½ head iceberg lettuce, chopped

The day before serving, separate the onion slices into individual rings, and place them in a large bowl, along with the pepperoni and the bleu cheese.

Add the oil and vinegar; season with the salt and pepper to taste.

Toss in the spinach and the lettuce, mixing well.

Cover the bowl, and chill the salad overnight.

Serves 6 to 8.

GAZPACHO SALAD

This salad contains the same ingredients as the popular cold Spanish soup. If you have a deep glass bowl, you can show this salad off to its best advantage.

---

2 cucumbers, peeled and finely chopped
4 tomatoes, coarsely chopped
2 green peppers, finely chopped
1 large onion, finely chopped
Salt and freshly ground pepper to taste
¼ cup wine or cider vinegar
½ cup olive oil
2 cloves garlic, crushed
Pinch of powdered cumin
1 tablespoon chopped parsley
2 scallions, finely chopped (white part only)
Seasoned croutons for garnish

Using a deep bowl, make alternate layers of the cucumbers, tomatoes, green peppers, and onion; season the layers with salt and pepper to taste.

In a small bowl, with a wire whisk, combine the vinegar, oil, garlic, cumin, parsley, and scallions; mix well.

Pour the dressing over the salad, cover the bowl, and chill well before serving.

Just before serving, garnish the salad with the croutons.

Serves 4.

ELEGANT RICE SALAD

2 packages (6 or 8 ounces each) chicken-flavored rice
2 jars (4 ounces each) marinated artichokes
½ cup pitted black olives, sliced
6 scallions, chopped
½ cup mayonnaise
Freshly ground pepper
½ cup diced pimientos

Prepare the rice according to the package directions. Let it cool to room temperature.

Drain the liquid from the artichokes into a large bowl; coarsely chop the artichoke hearts, and add them to the bowl.

Add the olives, scallions, mayonnaise, pepper, and the pimientos to the bowl.

Add the cooled rice, mixing well.

Refrigerate the salad for 4 to 5 hours before serving.

Serves 12.

MAGIC RICE SALAD

---

2 packages (6 ounces each) long grain and wild rice
½ pound fresh mushrooms, sliced
1 bunch scallions, chopped (including green tops)
1 cup oil-and-vinegar salad dressing

Prepare the rice according to the package directions, omitting the butter called for on the package.

Let the rice cool to room temperature; then add the mushrooms, scallions, and the salad dressing, mixing well.

This salad tastes best when served at room temperature; it can be left standing for several hours at room temperature, but any leftover salad should be refrigerated.

Serves 8.

HERRING SALAD

Another unusual salad, this one was devised by Shirley Rubin-stein, a New Jersey–based cooking teacher.

1 jar (6 ounces) herring in wine sauce, drained and sliced
1 Golden Delicious apple, peeled, cored, and finely
 chopped
1 cup finely sliced Bermuda onion
½ cup chopped pecans
½ pound fresh mushrooms, sliced (optional)

DRESSING:

1 cup sour cream
1 cup mayonnaise
3 tablespoons chopped red onion
2 tablespoons fresh dill weed (or 1 tablespoon dried)
2 tablespoons chopped parsley
1 tablespoon celery seed
1 head romaine lettuce or 1 pound fresh spinach,
 washed and well drained

Several hours before serving, combine the herring, apple, onion, pecans, and the optional mushrooms in a large bowl.

In a small bowl, combine the salad dressing ingredients, mixing well, and pour these over the salad mixture; chill for several hours.

A few minutes before serving, arrange the lettuce or spinach on a large serving platter or on several individual plates; spoon the salad on top.

Serves 4 to 6.

PEARS RENDSBURG

A German dish that goes especially well with various roasts.

---

1 can (16 ounces) pear halves, well drained
½ cup unseasoned bread crumbs
¼ cup whole or jellied cranberry sauce

Preheat the oven to 350°F.

Lightly dip the outside of the pear halves into the bread crumbs, and place them in a lightly greased baking dish.

Spoon 1 or 2 teaspoons of the cranberry sauce into the center of each pear half.

Bake for 10 to 15 minutes, or until the pears are hot.

Serves 4 to 6.

PINEAPPLE PICKLES

A sweet-and-pungent condiment that is nice to serve with roast pork, ham, or poultry.

---

1 can (29 ounces) pineapple chunks in heavy syrup
¾ cup cider vinegar
6 whole allspice berries
3 whole cloves
1 cinnamon stick
1 teaspoon powdered coriander

The day before serving, drain the pineapple chunks, reserving ¾ cup of the syrup.

Place the reserved syrup in a heavy saucepan along with the vinegar and the spices; cook, uncovered, for 15 minutes.

Add the pineapple chunks, and bring the mixture to a boil; simmer for 5 minutes longer.

Remove the saucepan from the heat, and let the mixture cool.

Pour the mixture into a large jar or container with a tight-fitting lid, and refrigerate for at least 24 hours.

Serve the pineapple chunks in their liquid (discard the whole spices) in an attractive crystal bowl.

Makes about 3 cups.

zucchini

wheat

pineapple

CHAPTER 4

BAKED GOODS

**Yeast Breads & Rolls
Quick Breads & Muffins
Cakes & Tortes
Cream Puffs & Cookies**

Yeast Breads & Rolls

CASALE ITALIAN BREAD

A cross between a pizza and a bread that can be served as a main dish.

---

2 envelopes dry yeast
2½ cups lukewarm water
1½ teaspoons sugar
1 tablespoon salt
½ cup olive oil
6 to 8 cups sifted flour
1 tablespoon oregano
1 pound mozzarella cheese, grated
1 pound pepperoni sausage, with casing removed, very thinly sliced
1 egg, beaten with 1 tablespoon water

In a large bowl, combine the yeast, 1 cup of the water, and ½ teaspoon of the sugar, and stir until the yeast is dissolved. Be careful that the water is not too hot, or it will kill the yeast.

Add the remaining water and sugar, as well as the salt and the olive oil.

Using an electric mixer at low speed, or a wooden spoon, gradually add 3 cups of the flour.

At this point, you should continue beating by hand, unless your mixer is equipped with a dough hook. Add 3 more cups of flour, beating to form a soft dough. If it is too sticky, more flour can be worked in later.

Turn the dough out onto a floured surface, and knead it to form a smooth ball, working in more flour if necessary.

Place the dough in an oiled bowl; cover the dough, and let it rise, away from drafts, until double in bulk.

Preheat the oven to 400°F.

Divide the dough in half, and roll each half out into a large rectangle.

Sprinkle each rectangle with the oregano and the grated cheese; arrange the sliced pepperoni on top of each rectangle.

Starting at the long edge, roll each rectangle up in jelly-roll fashion.

Shape rolls into horseshoes, and place them on lightly greased cookie sheets; brush the tops with the egg mixture.

Bake for 30 to 35 minutes, or until the bottom of the breads are lightly browned and they sound hollow when lightly tapped.

Let the breads cool for 10 minutes on a wire rack before serving.

Makes 2 loaves; each loaf serves 3 to 4.

Note: If desired, a variation of this bread can be made by altering the filling as follows: Sauté 1 to 1½ pounds of sweet Italian sausage, and drain well. Combine with 1 pound of grated provolone cheese and 1 large Spanish onion that has been chopped and sautéed. Use this mixture to fill the dough as directed above. Four small loaves can be made instead of two large ones. Bake them as directed above.

HINT

When making yeast bread on days with high humidity, the dough may require up to 1 cup more flour than the recipe calls for.

CALZONE

1 envelope dry yeast
1 teaspoon sugar
1 cup warm water
1 teaspoon salt
1 tablespoon olive oil
3 cups flour

FILLING #1:

½ pound mozzarella cheese, diced
¼ pound prosciutto ham, cut into ½-inch strips
1 tablespoon olive oil
Salt and pepper to taste

FILLING #2:

2 cups ricotta cheese, drained
½ to ¾ cup grated mozzarella cheese
¼ cup grated provolone or Parmesan cheese
½ teaspoon oregano
2 tablespoons cornmeal

To make the dough, sprinkle the yeast and the sugar over the warm water in a large bowl; stir, and wait until the mixture bubbles.

Stir in the salt, oil, and half of the flour; mix well by hand, or with an electric mixer at low speed.

With a wooden spoon, gradually beat in the remaining flour to make a soft dough. If it is too sticky, add a little more flour.

Turn the dough out onto a floured surface, and knead it until the dough is smooth and elastic.

Place the dough in a lightly oiled bowl, cover it, and let it rise away from drafts until it is double in bulk.

Meanwhile, prepare one of the desired fillings by combining all ingredients called for in a medium bowl; set aside.

Punch down the dough, and let it rest for 10 minutes.

Preheat the oven to 450°F.

Roll the dough out into 8 to 10 4-inch circles. (If you prefer, you can roll the dough out to form 1 large circle.)

Place about 2 tablespoons of the desired filling over one-half of each circle; fold it in half, and pinch the edges together to seal them well.

Brush a cookie sheet lightly with oil, and sprinkle the cornmeal on top. Place the calzones on the prepared cookie sheet, and bake them for 20 minutes.

Serve as a main dish, or as an accompaniment to pasta or salad.

Serves 4 to 6.

SIMPLY ELEGANT CROISSANTS

5 cups flour
1 cup firm butter
1 envelope dry yeast
1 cup warm water
¾ cup + 2 tablespoons evaporated milk
⅓ cup sugar
2 eggs, at room temperature
1½ teaspoons salt
¼ cup melted butter

Several hours or the day before baking, place 4 cups of the flour in a large bowl.

With a pastry blender, cut in the firm butter until the mixture resembles kidney beans.

In a medium bowl, combine the yeast and the warm water, stirring until the yeast is dissolved.

To the yeast mixture, add ¾ cup of the evaporated milk, the sugar, 1 egg, and the salt; beat well.

Add the remaining flour, mixing to form a smooth batter.

Add the melted butter, and pour this mixture over the butter-flour mixture in the large bowl; stir until all the flour is moistened, but do not overmix.

Cover the bowl, and refrigerate the dough for at least 2 hours. (It may be refrigerated for up to 4 days.)

About 3 hours before baking, remove the dough from the refrigerator, and knead it just 5 or 6 times on a well-floured surface to remove any air bubbles.

Divide the dough into fourths, and work with one fourth at a time, returning the remaining dough to the refrigerator (covered with foil or plastic wrap) until needed.

Roll each fourth into a 16-inch circle; the butter particles will be visible.

Cut the circle into 8 pie-shaped wedges, and roll each wedge from the widest end; curve it to form a crescent shape.

Place the croissants on an ungreased cookie sheet; repeat with the remaining three-fourths of the dough.

Let the croissants rise for 2 hours in a cool part of the kitchen, loosely covered with plastic wrap.

When the croissants are almost double in size, preheat the oven to 350°F.

Brush the tops of the croissants with a mixture of the remaining egg and evaporated milk.

Bake the croissants for 25 to 30 minutes, or until golden brown. Serve hot, or freeze them for future use.

Makes 32 croissants.

OLD FASHIONED OATMEAL–MOLASSES BREAD

1 cup rolled oats (old-fashioned or quick-cooking)
2 cups boiling water
½ cup light molasses
2 teaspoons salt
1 tablespoon butter or margarine
1 envelope dry yeast
½ cup lukewarm water
6 cups flour

Place the oats in a large bowl, and pour the boiling water on top; stir well, and let stand for 1 hour.

Add the molasses, salt, and the butter to the oatmeal.

In a small bowl, dissolve the yeast in the lukewarm water; when it has dissolved, stir it into the oatmeal mixture.

Stir in 4½ cups of the flour, beating well.

Cover the bowl with a towel, and let it rise, away from drafts, until the dough is double in bulk.

Add enough additional flour to form a smooth dough.

Knead the dough on a floured surface until it is smooth and elastic—about 5 minutes.

Form the dough into 2 loaves, and place them in 2 greased 9 × 5 × 3-inch loaf pans; cover the pans with oiled waxed paper, and let them stand until the loaves are double in bulk.

Preheat the oven to 350°F.

Bake the loaves for 50 minutes, or until they are golden brown on top; immediately turn the baked loaves out onto wire racks to cool.

Makes 2 loaves.

HINT

Never use oil to "grease" cake pans. Use solid shortening because oil can be absorbed into the batter as the cake bakes, causing sticking. Recipes call for greasing and flouring the pan because the flour helps prevent the fat from being absorbed into the batter.

Quick Breads & Muffins

OATMEAL QUICK BREAD

3 cups sifted flour
1¼ cups quick-cooking rolled oats (or 1½ cups
  old-fashioned oats)
1½ tablespoons baking powder
2 teaspoons salt
1 egg
¼ cup honey
1½ cups milk
1 tablespoon melted butter or margarine

Preheat the oven to 350°F.

In a large bowl, combine the flour with the oats, the baking powder, and the salt.

In a medium bowl, beat the egg with a wire whisk, and add the honey and the milk, mixing well.

Pour the egg mixture into the flour mixture, and stir just until the dry ingredients are moistened; the batter will be lumpy.

Turn the batter into a greased 9 × 5 × 3-inch loaf pan, and bake for 1¼ hours, or until the crust appears dry on top, and a knife inserted in the center comes out clean.

Turn the bread out of its pan onto a wire rack, and turn it right side up; brush the top with the melted butter.

Let the loaf cool for 10 minutes before slicing; or store in the refrigerator for future use.

Makes 1 loaf.

APRICOT–WALNUT QUICK BREAD

---

1 cup dried apricots
1½ cups boiling water
2½ cups sifted flour
1 tablespoon baking powder
½ teaspoon salt
1 egg
1 teaspoon vanilla
1 cup sugar
¼ cup salad oil
1 cup coarsely chopped walnuts

Using a scissors, cut the dried apricots into small pieces, and place them in a small bowl; add the boiling water, and set aside to cool.

Preheat the oven to 350°F.

Sift the flour, baking powder, and salt together onto a sheet of waxed paper, and set aside.

In a large bowl, combine the egg, vanilla, sugar, and oil, beating well with a wooden spoon.

Gradually add the apricot-water mixture, beating constantly.

Add the flour mixture all at once; beat only until smooth.

Stir in the walnuts.

Turn the batter into a greased 9 × 5 × 3-inch loaf pan, and bake for 1 hour, or until a knife inserted in the center comes out clean.

Let the bread cool in its pan on a wire rack for 10 minutes; then carefully remove the bread from the pan to cool completely.

Wrap the bread in foil, and refrigerate several hours before slicing.

Makes 1 loaf.

JALAPEÑO CORN BREAD

A marvelous accompaniment to chili or soups, this bread may be too hot for some tastes because the jalapeño peppers definitely pack a wallop! If you prefer a milder version, substitute plain canned chilis, or omit them altogether. This recipe yields a moist, puddinglike bread.

3½ cups yellow cornmeal
2½ cups milk
½ cup salad oil
3 eggs
1 large onion, finely chopped
1 cup canned cream-style corn
1½ cups grated cheddar or Monterey Jack cheese
1 can (4 ounces) jalapeño peppers, drained

Preheat the oven to 400°F.

In a large bowl, combine the cornmeal with the milk and oil.

Beat the eggs, and add them to the bowl, along with the onion, corn, and the cheese.

Rinse the jalapeños in cold water, drain them on paper towels, and chop them finely; add them to the batter.

Pour the batter into a well oiled 13 × 9 × 2-inch baking pan, and bake for 45 minutes, or until a knife inserted in the center comes out clean.

If desired, you can spread the top with melted butter before cutting the bread into squares. Serve hot.

Serves 10 to 12.

ICE CREAM MUFFINS

This recipe won a "Bake Off" contest when I was much younger, and it has remained a favorite of mine.

---

1 cup vanilla ice cream, softened
1 cup self-rising flour

Preheat the oven to 425°F.

Grease a muffin tin, or line it with paper cupcake liners.

Combine the ice cream with the flour, and pour the mixture into the prepared tins or liners, filling each about three-quarters full.

Bake for 12 to 15 minutes; let the muffins cool slightly on a wire rack before serving.

Makes 6 to 8 muffins.

Cakes & Tortes

NEW YORK–STYLE CHEESECAKE

Also known as Lindy's Cheesecake (after that famed New York restaurant), this is for people who love a heavy cheesecake.

5 packages (8 ounces each) cream cheese, softened
1¾ cups sugar
3 tablespoons flour
Juice of 1 lemon
Grated peel of 1 lemon
½ teaspoon vanilla
5 eggs
2 egg yolks
½ cup sour cream
1 tablespoon softened butter or margarine
½ cup graham cracker crumbs

Preheat the oven to 350°F.

In a large bowl, with electric mixer at medium speed, beat the cream cheese until it is fluffy.

Slowly add the sugar, and beat until the mixture is light and fluffy.

Add the flour, lemon juice, lemon peel, and the vanilla; mix well.

Add the 5 eggs, and then the 2 egg yolks, 1 at a time, beating well after each addition; fold in the sour cream.

Rub the butter over the bottom of a 9- or 10-inch spring-form pan, and sprinkle the graham cracker crumbs on top.

Pour in the cheese mixture, and bake for 10 to 12 minutes.

Reduce the oven temperature to 200°F, and bake for 1 hour. Turn off the oven, and let the cake cool in the oven.

Refrigerate the cheesecake well before serving. Just before serving, remove the sides of the springform pan.

A fruit topping may be added if desired, but it is not necessary.

Serves 10 to 12.

THE ULTIMATE CHOCOLATE CHEESECAKE

Serve this cake when you feel like abandoning caution—and diets—to the winds!

---

1 cup chocolate cookie crumbs (made from chocolate
   wafers)
¼ teaspoon cinnamon
½ cup unsalted melted butter, slightly cooled
1 cup sugar
4 large eggs
3 packages (8 ounces each) cream cheese, softened
16 squares (1 ounce each) semisweet chocolate
1 teaspoon vanilla
2 tablespoons unsweetened cocoa
3 cups sour cream, at room temperature

The day before serving, prepare the crust by combining the chocolate crumbs with the cinnamon and ¼ cup of the melted butter. Press the mixture into the bottom of a 10-inch spring-form pan, and chill for 1 hour.

Preheat the oven to 425°F.

In a large bowl, with electric mixer at medium speed, beat together the sugar and the eggs until the mixture is light and fluffy.

Add the cream cheese gradually, beating well after each addition.

In the top part of a double boiler, over hot water, melt the chocolate, and let it cool; add cooled chocolate to the egg mixture.

With the electric mixer at low speed, add the vanilla, the cocoa, and the remaining melted butter; mix well.

Pour the batter into the chilled crust, and place the spring-form pan on a cookie sheet, and bake it for 55 minutes; the center will be soft.

Let the cake cool slightly on a wire rack. Then cover the top with 2 pieces of paper towel, and seal it with aluminum foil; this will prevent the top from hardening.

Refrigerate the cake in its pan overnight. Just before serving, remove the sides of the pan.

Serves 16 to 20.

HINT

When substituting whipped butter or margarine for the regular variety, use one-third to one-half more than the recipe calls for if the measurement is by volume (e.g., 1 cup, etc.). Use the same amount if the measurement is by weight (1/4 pound, etc.).

CHOCOLATE MOUSSE CAKE

Another sinfully rich offering for "chocoholics."

CAKE:

> ½ cup unsweetened cocoa
> ¾ cup boiling water
> 1¾ cups sifted cake flour
> Pinch of salt
> 1¾ cups sugar
> 1½ teaspoons baking soda
> ½ cup salad oil
> 7 egg yolks
> 2 teaspoons vanilla
> 8 egg whites, at room temperature
> ½ teaspoon cream of tartar

CHOCOLATE MOUSSE FILLING:

> 3 cups whipping cream
> 1½ cups sifted confectioners' sugar
> ¾ cup unsweetened cocoa
> 1½ teaspoons vanilla
> ½ teaspoon rum
> Pinch of salt
> 1 teaspoon unflavored gelatin
> 2 tablespoons cold water

Several hours before serving, prepare the cake: Preheat the oven to 325°F.

Place the cocoa in a small bowl; add the boiling water, stirring until smooth. Cool for about 20 minutes.

In another bowl, place the flour, salt, sugar, and the baking soda. Make a well in the center, and pour in the oil, egg yolks, the vanilla, and the cooled cocoa.

With an electric mixer at medium speed, beat this mixture until smooth; thoroughly wash and dry the beaters.

Sprinkle the cream of tartar over the egg whites in another large bowl.

Starting with the electric mixer at low speed, beat the egg whites until they foam; continue beating at high speed until they are very stiff.

Pour the cocoa mixture over the egg whites, gently folding them together with a rubber spatula just until blended.

Pour the batter into an ungreased 10-inch tube pan (angel cake pan), and bake for 60 minutes.

Place the pan on a wire rack for 5 minutes; then invert it over the neck of a bottle to allow the cake to cool completely. (This prevents the cake from collapsing as it cools.)

Meanwhile, prepare the chocolate mousse filling: Place the whipping cream in a large bowl, and chill it until it is very cold—about 30 minutes.

Add the sugar, cocoa, vanilla, rum, and a pinch of salt; with electric mixer at high speed, beat the cream mixture until it is stiff, and then return it to the refrigerator.

Sprinkle the gelatin over the 2 tablespoons of cold water to soften it.

Place the mixture in a small saucepan over hot water, and cook, stirring, until the gelatin is dissolved; remove it from the heat, and let it cool.

When the cake has cooled thoroughly, remove it from its pan, and prepare it for filling.

Cut a 1-inch slice crosswise from the top of the cake, and set it aside.

With a sharp knife, outline a well in the cake, being careful to leave ¾-inch-thick walls around the center hole and the sides.

With a spoon, carefully remove the cake from this area, being sure to leave a 1-inch base.

Crumble the cake you have just removed, and reserve 1½ cups. (Any leftover crumbled cake can be used for "nibbling.")

Measure 2½ cups of the chocolate whipped cream into a small bowl, and fold in the cooled gelatin; use this mixture to fill the well you made in the cake.

Replace the top slice over the cake.

Mix ½ cup of the chocolate whipped cream with the reserved 1½ cups of crumbled cake; use this to fill the hole in the center of the cake.

Frost the top and sides of the cake with the remaining chocolate whipped cream, and refrigerate the cake until serving.

Serves 12 to 15.

HINT

Separate eggs while they are still cold, but allow the whites to warm up to room temperature before beating them. Egg yolks, however, should not be left standing at room temperature for extended periods of time.

DIVINE CHOCOLATE

For those who cannot get enough of rich chocolate desserts, here is another from my special collection of chocolate recipes.

CAKE:

1 package (23 ounces) brownie mix (without nuts)
2 tablespoons water
3 eggs

FILLING:

4 cups (2 12-ounce packages) semisweet chocolate morsels
½ cup strong brewed coffee
3 eggs, separated
½ cup coffee liqueur
3 tablespoons sugar
½ cup whipping cream

GLAZE:

8 squares (1 ounce each) semisweet chocolate
⅓ cup water

Several hours before serving, prepare the cake: Preheat the oven to 350°F.

Combine the brownie mix with the water and eggs, in a medium bowl.

Grease and flour an 11 × 15-inch jelly-roll pan, and line the pan with parchment or waxed paper; lightly grease the paper.

Spread the batter over the paper, and bake it for 10 to 12 minutes.

Invert the cake onto a dish towel, and peel the paper off the bottom of the cake. Let the cake cool while you prepare the filling.

In a large, heavy saucepan, over low heat, melt the chocolate with the coffee, remove it from the heat, and let it cool well.

In a large bowl, beat the egg yolks until thick and lemony; stir in the cooled chocolate mixture.

Gradually add the coffee liqueur.

In a medium bowl, with the electric mixer at high speed, beat the egg whites until soft peaks form; gradually add the sugar, and continue beating until the egg whites are stiff and shiny.

In another bowl, with electric mixer at high speed, whip the cream until stiff peaks form.

With a rubber scraper, gently fold the whipped cream and the egg-white mixture into the chocolate mixture, and chill it for about 30 minutes.

To assemble the cake, lightly oil a 2-quart charlotte mold.

With a sharp knife, cut out 2 circles from the cake: one should fit the bottom of the mold, and the other should be big enough to fit the top of the mold after you have filled it.

Insert the smaller circle into the bottom of the mold. Cut up the remaining cake, and fit the pieces around the sides of the mold.

Spoon the filling into the mold, and cover it with the other circle of cake; chill the cake for 3 to 4 hours, or until the filling is firm.

At the last minute prepare the glaze: Heat the chocolate with the water in a heavy saucepan over low heat until the chocolate has melted; stir until the mixture is smooth.

Unmold the cake onto a serving platter, and spread the glaze on top, letting it drizzle down the sides as well.

Serves 12 to 15.

CHOCOLATE CREAM SLICES

Well worth the preparation time!

CAKE:

   ½ cup (3 ounces) semisweet chocolate morsels
   4 eggs, separated
   ⅛ teaspoon cream of tartar
   ½ cup sugar
   ¾ cup unsalted butter, softened
   ½ cup sifted flour

FILLING:

   1½ cups whipping cream
   1½ cups (9 ounces) semisweet chocolate morsels
   ¼ cup light rum
   1 teaspoon vanilla

GLAZE:

   1 cup sugar
   ⅓ cup water
   1 cup (6 ounces) semisweet chocolate pieces

To prepare the cake, preheat the oven to 350°F.

Place the chocolate in the top part of a double boiler, and melt it over hot, not boiling, water, stirring. Let the melted chocolate cool.

In a medium bowl, with electric mixer at high speed, beat the egg whites and the cream of tartar until soft peaks form.

Slowly add ¼ cup of the sugar, and continue beating until the egg whites are stiff and shiny. Set the egg whites aside. (By beating the egg whites before you beat the cake batter, you do not have to wash and dry the beaters before proceeding with the rest of the recipe.)

In a large bowl, with electric mixer at medium speed, cream

the butter and the remaining sugar until it is light and fluffy.

Add the egg yolks and the cooled chocolate, beating well.

With a rubber scraper, carefully fold in the beaten egg whites, blending thoroughly; then fold in the flour, blending well.

Spread the batter over a greased and floured 11 × 15-inch jelly-roll pan, and bake for 12 to 15 minutes, or until the cake shrinks slightly from the sides of the pan.

Remove the cake from the oven, and cool it in its pan for 15 minutes; then turn the cake out onto a large cake rack to cool thoroughly.

Meanwhile, prepare the filling. Combine the cream and the chocolate in a medium saucepan, and cook over medium heat, stirring constantly, until the mixture thickens.

Pour the mixture into a large bowl, and refrigerate it for at least an hour.

When the mixture is thoroughly chilled, add the rum and vanilla, and with electric mixer at high speed, whip the cream until soft peaks form when the beaters are raised from the bowl.

Cut the cake in half to form 2 11 × 7½-inch layers. Place one layer on a serving platter, and spread the filling on top.

Place the second layer over the filling, and chill the cake for 1 hour.

Prepare the glaze by combining the sugar, water, and the chocolate in a small saucepan; cook, stirring constantly, over medium heat until the sugar has dissolved, and the chocolate is melted.

Remove the saucepan from the heat, and let it stand, covered, for about 20 minutes.

Carefully spoon the glaze evenly over the top of the cake, letting it drizzle down the sides as well.

Return the cake to the refrigerator until serving. To serve, cut the cake into small slices.

Serves 12 to 15.

CHOCOLATE GATEAU

After fifteen years, this is still one of my most treasured recipes.

CAKE:

½ cup + 2 teaspoons unsalted butter, softened
⅔ cup semisweet chocolate morsels
2 tablespoons dark rum
⅔ cup + 2 tablespoons sugar
3 eggs, separated
Pinch of salt
⅓ cup finely ground blanched almonds
½ teaspoon almond extract
¾ cup sifted cake flour

ICING:

1 cup butter or margarine, softened
1 pound sifted confectioners' sugar
3 egg yolks
3 ounces dark sweet chocolate, melted and cooled
1 tablespoon dark rum

Preheat the oven to 350°F; rub the inside of an 8-inch spring-form pan with 2 teaspoons of the softened butter.

In the top part of a double boiler, over hot water, melt the chocolate with the rum; remove the pan from the heat, and let the chocolate cool.

In a large bowl, with electric mixer at medium speed, cream the remaining butter with ⅔ cup of the sugar until it is soft and fluffy—at least 5 minutes.

Add the egg yolks one at a time, beating well after each addition.

Thoroughly wash and dry the beaters, and in a medium bowl, with electric mixer at high speed, beat the egg whites until they begin to hold peaks.

Slowly add the remaining sugar, and continue beating until the whites are stiff and shiny; set them aside.

Add the cooled chocolate to the butter mixture; then fold in the almonds, the almond extract, and the flour.

With a rubber scraper, gently fold in the egg whites, blending well.

Spoon the batter into the prepared pan, and bake for 25 to 30 minutes, or until the cake springs back when gently poked with your finger.

Let the cake cool in its pan for 15 minutes; then remove the sides of the springform pan, and let the cake cool on a wire rack for about 2 hours before icing it.

To prepare the icing, in a large bowl, with electric mixer at medium speed, cream the butter until it is soft.

Gradually add the confectioners' sugar, beating well to blend it in with the butter.

Add the egg yolks one at a time, beating well after each addition; stir in the cooled melted chocolate and the rum, mixing well.

Use this mixture to frost the tops and sides of the gateau, making swirl designs with a spatula.

Any remaining icing can be piped through a pastry tube to make decorative piping and/or rosettes on top.

Serves 12.

BEST POUND CAKE EVER

1 cup butter or margarine, softened
3 cups sugar
6 eggs
3 cups sifted flour
¼ teaspoon baking soda
1 cup sour cream

Preheat the oven to 300°F; grease and flour a 10-inch tube or Bundt pan.

In a large bowl, with electric mixer at medium speed, cream the butter and the sugar until light and fluffy.

Add the eggs one at a time, beating well after each addition.

Sift the flour and baking soda together, and with the electric mixer at low speed, add the flour mixture to the bowl alternately with the sour cream, beginning and ending with the flour mixture.

Pour the batter into the prepared pan, and bake it for 1½ to 2 hours, or until a knife inserted in the center comes out clean.

Let the cake cool in its pan on a wire rack for about 1 hour before removing it from the pan to cool thoroughly.

Serves 12.

If you add 2 tablespoons of boiling water to a butter-sugar mixture that you are creaming, you will have a finer-textured cake.

It is not necessary to grease the sides of a cake pan. Batter cannot cling to slippery sides; so it will not rise as high. You can always loosen baked cake from the sides of a pan by running a knife around the edges.

Altering the size of a cake pan indicated in any recipe affects both the baking time and the volume of the cake; so it's not a good idea to deviate.

Tests for doneness vary with the kinds of cake you are baking. In general, you can test a layer cake (from a mix or from scratch) or a pound cake by inserting a knife, a broom straw, or a wire cake-tester in the center; if it comes out clean, the cake is done. With a sponge cake (one with a lot of beaten eggs or egg whites), the best test for doneness is to touch it lightly with your finger; it should spring back readily. In both cases, a cake that is fully baked will shrink slightly from the sides of the pan.

PINEAPPLE POUND CAKE

½ cup vegetable shortening
1 cup butter or margarine, softened
2¾ cups sugar
6 eggs
3 cups flour
1 teaspoon baking powder
¼ cup milk mixed with 1 teaspoon vanilla
1 can (15 ounces) crushed pineapple
¼ cup melted butter or margarine
1½ cups sifted confectioners' sugar

In a large bowl, with electric mixer at medium speed, cream the shortening with the softened butter and the sugar until the mixture is light and fluffy.

Add the eggs one at a time, beating well after each addition.

Combine the flour and the baking powder in a 4-cup measuring cup, and add it to the creamed mixture alternately with the milk mixture; stir well with a wooden spoon after each addition.

Measure ¾ cup of crushed pineapple along with some of the juice from the can, and add it to the batter. (Drain the juice off from the remaining pineapple, and set aside the pineapple for the glaze.)

Pour the batter into a well-greased 10-inch tube or Bundt pan.

Place the cake pan in a cold oven, and set the temperature to 325°F.

Bake the cake for 1¼ hours, or until the cake tests done.

Cool the cake in its pan on a wire rack for 30 minutes; then invert the cake onto a serving platter, and let it cool thoroughly.

To prepare the glaze, combine the melted margarine with the sugar, mixing until smooth.

Stir in the reserved pineapple, and drizzle this mixture over the top and sides of the cake.

Serves 16 to 20.

HINT

This and other recipes in this book call for canned pineapple, which lends itself to cooking better than the fresh variety. The latter is delicious when served just as is. To store fresh pineapple properly, don't subject it to temperature changes. If it was chilled when you bought it at the store, keep it chilled at home. If the store kept it at room temperature, you should do the same at home. This prevents the pineapple from developing the dark spots that result from temperature changes.

WALNUT APPLE CAKE

---

4 cups peeled and coarsely chopped apples
2 cups sugar
2 eggs
½ cup salad oil
2 teaspoons vanilla
2 cups flour
2 teaspoons baking soda
1 teaspoon salt
2 teaspoons cinnamon
1 cup chopped walnuts

Preheat the oven to 350°F; grease a 10-inch tube or Bundt pan.

Combine the apples and sugar in a medium bowl, and set them aside.

In a large bowl, with a wire whisk, beat the eggs for 1 minute; add the oil and the vanilla.

Sift together the flour, baking soda, salt, and cinnamon into a 4-cup measuring cup.

Add the flour mixture to the eggs alternately with the apple-sugar mixture, stirring well with a wooden spoon after each addition.

Stir in the walnuts, and pour the batter into the prepared pan; bake it for 1 hour, or until the cake tests done.

Cook the cake in its pan on a wire rack for 15 minutes; then invert the cake onto a wire rack to cool thoroughly.

Serves 12 to 15.

HINT

Know your apples: Winesaps, Cortlands, McIntoshes, Staymans, and Jonathans are all-purpose apples for use in salads, cakes, applesauce, or for eating out of hand. Romes are great baking apples. Delicious apples are for salads or for eating fresh. Although any tart variety can be used for apple pies, Northern Spy is the best.

JEWISH APPLE CAKE

*This seems to be the recipe for which I receive the most re-
quests from all over the country!*

---

4 to 6 firm apples, peeled and sliced
2 teaspoons cinnamon
2¼ cups sugar
3 cups flour
1 tablespoon baking powder
1 cup salad oil
4 eggs
⅓ cup orange juice
½ teaspoon salt
2½ teaspoons vanilla

Preheat the oven to 350°F, and grease and flour a 10-inch
tube or Bundt pan.

In a medium bowl, combine the apples with the cinnamon
and ¼ cup of the sugar; set aside.

In a large bowl, with electric mixer at medium speed, combine the remaining sugar, the flour, baking powder, oil, eggs,
orange juice, salt, and the vanilla; beat until the batter is
smooth.

Pour a small amount of the batter into the prepared pan,
and place a layer of the apple slices on top.

Continue layering in this fashion, ending with a layer of
batter.

Bake the cake for 1½ hours, or until it tests done.

Cool the cake in its pan for 30 minutes on a wire rack; then
turn the cake out onto the rack to cool thoroughly.

Serves 16 to 20.

MACADAMIA NUT–CARROT CAKE

3 eggs
2 cups sugar
1½ cups salad oil
2 teaspoons vanilla
1 can (8½ ounces) crushed pineapple, undrained
2 cups grated raw carrot
3 cups cake flour
1 teaspoon baking powder
1 teaspoon baking soda
1 teaspoon salt
1 teaspoon cinnamon
1 teaspoon nutmeg
1 cup chopped macadamia nuts

Preheat the oven to 350°F, and grease and flour a 10-inch tube or Bundt pan.

In a large bowl, with electric mixer at medium speed, beat together the eggs, sugar, and the oil until well blended.

With the electric mixer at low speed, add the vanilla, the pineapple (and its juice) and the grated carrots.

Sift together the flour with the baking powder, baking soda, salt, cinnamon, and the nutmeg; sift the dry ingredients together 2 more times.

With the electric mixer at low speed, slowly add the dry ingredients to the bowl, beating until well blended.

Stir in the nuts, and blend thoroughly.

Spoon the batter into the prepared pan, and bake for 1¼ hours, or until the cake tests done.

Let the cake cool in its pan on a wire rack for 30 minutes; then turn the cake out onto a wire rack to cool thoroughly.

If desired, the cake can be dusted with confectioners' sugar or spread with any cream cheese frosting; but it is also quite moist and flavorful when served plain.

Serves 12 to 15.

BANANA WALNUT CAKE

A food processor makes this recipe child's play, but it's equally easy to prepare using an electric mixer. Fix this any time you have some overripe bananas to use up.

---

3 ripe bananas
½ cup walnuts
½ cup sugar
1 teaspoon salt
2 eggs
1½ cups flour
1¼ teaspoons baking soda
¼ cup melted butter or margarine

Preheat the oven to 350°F.

Using a food processor fitted with the steel blade, combine the bananas and the walnuts, processing until the bananas are mashed and the walnuts are chopped.

With the motor still running, add the sugar, salt, and the eggs through the feed tube, mixing well.

Combine the flour with the baking soda, and add it to the banana mixture (in three parts) alternately with the melted butter (in two parts), processing well after each addition.

Pour the batter into a greased 8-inch tube pan, a Kugelhof mold, or a 9 × 5 × 3-inch loaf pan, and bake for about 40 to 45 minutes, or until nicely browned on top.

Cool the cake in its pan on a wire rack for 30 minutes; then invert the cake onto a serving plate, and dust with confectioners' sugar, if desired.

Serves 8.

LEMON ANGEL CAKE

With a recipe like this, no one will notice that it was made using convenience foods.

---

1 package (14½ ounces) angel food cake mix
1 package (3 ounces) noninstant lemon pudding and
  pie-filling mix
½ cup sugar
2 egg yolks
2 tablespoons lemon juice
1 tablespoon grated lemon peel
2½ cups whipping cream
1 package (12 or 16 ounces) flaked coconut

The day before serving, prepare the angel cake mix according to the package directions, and bake it in a 10-inch angel cake pan as directed.

Let the cake cool in its pan inverted over the neck of a bottle.

Meanwhile, prepare the pudding mix as directed on the package for lemon meringue pie filling, using the ½ cup of sugar and 2 egg yolks, but reducing the amount of water called for to 2 cups.

When the lemon pudding mixture has thickened, remove it from the heat, and stir in the lemon juice and grated lemon peel; pour the mixture into a medium bowl, and refrigerate, covered, for about 1 hour.

In a large bowl, with electric mixer at high speed, whip 1 cup of the cream until soft peaks form; fold one-half of the flaked coconut into the whipped cream. (Set the other half aside until the next day; also keep the remaining whipping cream cold until the next day.)

Fold the coconut–whipped cream mixture into the cooled pudding.

To assemble the cake, split it horizontally into 4 or 5 layers, using a sharp knife.

Place the bottom layer on a plate, and spread about 1 cup of the lemon–whipped cream mixture on top.

Place another cake layer over the filling, and spread with another cup of the mixture; repeat the process, using all the cake layers and filling, and ending with a layer of cake on top.

Cover the cake, and refrigerate it overnight.

The next day, several hours before serving, in a large bowl, with electric mixer at high speed, whip the remaining 1½ cups of whipping cream until soft peaks form.

Fold in the remaining coconut, and use this mixture to frost the top and sides of the cake.

Return the cake to the refrigerator, and chill for several hours.

Serves 12 to 15.

EASY BUT ELEGANT TORTE

1 cup flour
1 cup chopped walnuts or pecans
½ cup butter or margarine, softened
1 container (8 ounces) frozen whipped topping, thawed
1 cup sifted confectioners' sugar
1 package (8 ounces) cream cheese, softened
1 package (3 ounces) instant vanilla pudding mix
1 package (3 ounces) instant chocolate pudding mix
2 cups milk
1 chocolate candy bar (2¼ ounces), frozen

Several hours or the day before serving, preheat the oven to 350°F.

In a medium bowl, combine the flour, chopped nuts, and the butter; press this mixture into the bottom of a 9 × 13 × 2-inch baking pan.

Bake the crust for 15 to 20 minutes; let it cool on a wire rack.

In a medium bowl, with a wooden spoon, combine 1 cup of the whipped topping with the confectioners' sugar and the softened cream cheese; blend well.

Spread this mixture over the cooled crust.

In a large bowl, wtih electric mixer at medium speed, beat together both instant puddings with the milk until the mixture is thick and creamy; spread this mixture over the cream cheese layer.

Spread the remaining whipped topping over the pudding layer; grate the frozen chocolate bar, and sprinkle it over the whipped topping.

Refrigerate the torte, covered, for several hours or overnight. To serve, cut into squares.

Serves 10 to 12.

TARTE JEAN–PAUL

Superb and deliciously different, from Chef Jean-Paul of Jean-Paul's Restaurant in Milwaukee, Wisconsin.

1½ cups sifted flour
Pinch of salt
2 tablespoons sugar, optional (if a sweeter dough is desired)
½ cup butter, softened
¼ cup ice water (approximately)
2 packages (3 ounces each) cream cheese
¾ cup sugar
3 eggs
1 cup whipping cream
1 teaspoon vanilla
¼ cup Cointreau or orange liqueur
Grated peel of ½ lemon
Cinnamon for topping

Preheat the oven to 400°F.

Prepare the dough: Combine the flour, salt, and the optional sugar and the butter, either by using a food processor or by rubbing the ingredients together between your fingers, until all the butter is absorbed, and the mixture resembles cornmeal.

Add just enough ice water to bind the mixture into a dough, tossing with a fork.

Turn the dough out onto a floured surface; with the palm of your hand, push the dough down and away from you, and then bring it back into a ball. Repeat this process 2 or 3 times.

The dough should be soft at this stage; if it is too sticky, wrap it in waxed paper, and chill it. Otherwise, it is ready to be rolled out.

Butter and flour a 10-inch flan ring or quiche pan.

Roll out the dough to ⅛-inch thickness, and fit it into the prepared pan.

Line the dough with parchment or waxed paper, and fill it with pie weights or dried beans; bake the dough for 8 to 10 minutes.

Meanwhile, in a medium bowl with electric mixer at medium speed, combine the cream cheese with the sugar.

Add the eggs one at a time, beating well after each addition.

With the mixer running at low speed, slowly add the cream, vanilla, the Cointreau, and the grated lemon peel.

After the *tarte* shell has baked for 8 to 10 minutes, remove it from the oven; remove the paper and the weights or beans.

Fill the shell with the cheese mixture, and return it to the oven to bake at 400°F for about 35 minutes, or until the filling is set and golden brown.

Sprinkle the *tarte* with a little cinnamon, and let it cool on a wire rack. Serve the *tarte* at room temperature or chilled.

Serves 8 to 10.

HINT

Never work pastry dough more than is necessary, as it will become difficult to roll out, and the baked dough will be tough. The reason is that overhandling releases the gluten in the flour, giving the dough extra elasticity. This is fine for bread dough but not desirable for delicate pastry doughs.

SCHWARZWALDER TORTE

TORTE:

    5 egg whites, at room temperature
    ½ cup sugar
    3 tablespoons flour
    1 cup finely chopped toasted almonds or hazlenuts

ICING:

    1 cup (6 ounces) semisweet chocolate
    ¼ cup water
    ½ teaspoon powdered instant coffee

FILLING:

    1½ cups whipping cream
    5 tablespoons confectioners' sugar
    2 tablespoons kirsch or cognac
    For garnish: grated sweet chocolate or chocolate curls

Several hours before serving, preheat the oven to 425°F. Lightly grease and flour 2 large cookie sheets.

In a large bowl, with the electric mixer at high speed, beat the egg whites until stiff peaks form.

Combine the sugar with the flour, and gradually fold this mixture into the egg whites; fold in the chopped nuts, blending well.

With an 8-inch pie plate as a guide, use your finger to trace 4 8-inch circles on the prepared cookie sheets; spread each circle evenly with the egg white mixture.

Bake the meringue circles for 5 to 10 minutes, or until they are light brown. (They will be very soft.)

Remove the circles with a spatula or a sharp knife to cake racks to cool.

Meanwhile, prepare the icing: Combine the chocolate, water, and powdered coffee in the top part of a double boiler.

Heat the mixture over hot, not boiling, water, stirring occasionally, until the chocolate has melted and the mixture is smooth.

Spread the icing thinly over the meringues, and let them set for several hours.

About one-half hour before serving, place the cream, sugar, and kirsch or cognac in a large bowl; with the electric mixer at high speed, whip the mixture until stiff peaks form.

To assemble the torte, place one meringue circle on a serving plate, and spread with some of the whipped cream. Repeat with the remaining layers and whipped cream, leaving enough to cover the top and the sides of the torte.

Decorate the top with the chocolate curls or grated chocolate; if not serving the torte right away, keep it well chilled.

Serves 8 to 10.

TEXAS DOUBLE–FROSTED BOURBON BROWNIES

BROWNIES:

¾ cup flour
¼ teaspoon baking powder
¼ teaspoon salt
½ cup sugar
2 tablespoons water
1 cup (6 ounces) semisweet chocolate morsels
1 teaspoon vanilla
⅓ cup vegetable shortening or margarine
2 eggs
1½ cups chopped walnuts or pecans
2 tablespoons bourbon

FROSTING:

½ cup unsalted butter, softened
1 teaspoon vanilla
2 cups sifted confectioners' sugar
1 tablespoon shortening or margarine
1 cup (6 ounces) semisweet chocolate morsels

Preheat the oven to 325°F; grease and flour a 9 × 9 × 2-inch baking pan.

Sift the flour, baking powder, and salt together onto a sheet of waxed paper; set aside.

In a medium saucepan, combine the sugar and the water, and bring it to a boil; boil for 1 to 2 minutes, and then remove the pan from the heat.

Add the chocolate, vanilla, and the shortening, stirring until the mixture is smooth and has cooled to lukewarm.

Beat in the eggs; then slowly add the flour mixture, beating well with a wire whisk.

Stir in the nuts with a wooden spoon, and turn the batter into the prepared pan.

Bake the brownies for 25 to 30 minutes.

Remove the pan from the oven, and immediately sprinkle the bourbon on top; let the pan cool on a wire rack.

Meanwhile, prepare the frosting: In a medium bowl, with electric mixer at medium speed, cream the butter and the vanilla until the mixture is smooth.

Gradually add the confectioners' sugar, beating well.

Use this mixture to frost the cooled brownies.

In the top part of a double boiler, over hot water, melt the shortening with the chocolate; let cool slightly.

Spread the chocolate glaze over the white frosting, and chill the brownies well.

To serve, cut into squares.

Serves 8 to 10.

BAKLAVA

2 cups (approximately) peanut oil or melted Greek
    butter, if available
1 pound filo pastry
3 to 4 cups coarsely chopped almonds (do not blanch
    them)
1 cup sugar combined with 2 tablespoons cinnamon

SYRUP:

3 cups sugar
1½ cups water
Juice of ½ lemon
Rind of 1 lemon
Rind of 1 orange
1 cinnamon stick

Preheat the oven to 350°F.

With a pastry brush, coat the bottom and sides of a 13 × 9
× 2-inch baking pan with about 2 tablespoons of the oil or
melted butter.

Place 1 sheet of filo into the prepared pan, and brush it
thoroughly with the oil or butter.

Lay another sheet of filo on top, and brush in the same
manner; repeat the process until you have used 5 sheets.

Sprinkle the fifth filo sheet with about 3 tablespoons of the
chopped almonds and 1 tablespoon of the sugar-cinnamon
mixture.

Place another sheet of filo on top, and brush it with oil or
butter.

Top with another sheet of filo, and sprinkle with about 3
tablespoons of the chopped almonds and 1 tablespoon of the
sugar-cinnamon mixture.

Repeat the procedure, spreading the filo sheets alternately
with the nuts and sugar, and then with the oil or butter, until
you have only 5 filo sheets left.

The last 5 filo sheets should be buttered only, as you did with the first 5, except you should leave the final sheet dry. Sprinkle this one with cold water.

Bake the baklava for 45 minutes.

Remove the pan from the oven, and place it on a wire rack to cool slightly.

With a sharp knife, cut diagonally two thirds of the way down to the bottom, first in one direction and then in the other, to form diamonds.

Meanwhile, prepare the syrup by combining the sugar, water, lemon juice, lemon rind, orange rind, and the cinnamon stick in a large saucepan.

Bring to a boil, and cook for 10 minutes. Let the syrup cool, and then discard the lemon and orange rind, and the cinnamon stick.

Pour the syrup over the baklava, and chill it for 1 or more hours.

Just before serving, finish cutting the diamonds all the way down to the bottom, so that the pieces can be easily removed.

Makes about 2½ dozen; serves 12 to 15.

Cream Puffs & Cookies

BASIC CREAM PUFF DOUGH

A very serviceable recipe that can be used in a variety of dessert recipes, as well as in making hors d'oeuvres.

---

1 cup water
½ cup butter or margarine
¼ teaspoon salt
1 cup flour
4 eggs

Preheat the oven to 400°F.

In a heavy saucepan, combine the water, butter, and salt, and bring it to a boil over high heat.

Remove the pan from the heat and, with a wooden spoon, beat in the flour all at once.

Reduce the heat to low, return the saucepan to the heat, and continue cooking the mixture, stirring constantly, until it forms a ball in the center of the saucepan.

Remove the pan from the heat, and add the eggs one at a time, beating vigorously after each addition, until the dough is smooth, and all the eggs are absorbed.

Continue beating until the mixture is shiny and forms "ribbons" when the spoon is lifted from the pan.

Bake on ungreased cookie sheets as follows:

For *miniature* cream puffs, drop by teaspoonfuls, and bake for 15 to 18 minutes, or until the dough is puffy and golden brown.

For *regular-size* cream puffs, drop by tablespoonfuls, and bake for 35 to 40 minutes, or until puffed and golden brown.

For *eclairs*, drop by tablespoonfuls, 3 inches apart, and shape the dough into 4 × 1-inch strips with a spatula. Bake for 35 to 40 minutes.

Regardless of the size or shape of the puffs you make, as soon as you remove them from the oven, make a small gash in the sides of each one with a paring knife, to allow the steam to escape.

Then let the puffs cool thoroughly on a wire rack. Unfilled puffs can be stored in a cool, dry place for up to 2 days, or they can be frozen.

Make about 5 dozen miniature cream puffs or 1½ dozen larger puffs.

SUGGESTED FILLINGS:

Vanilla or chocolate pudding, any flavor ice cream, slightly sweetened whipped cream. If desired, drizzle a chocolate glaze or chocolate sauce on top.

STRAWBERRY (OR CHERRY) CHOCOLATE CHIP COOKIES

1 package (18½ ounces) strawberry- or cherry-flavored
   cake mix
¼ cup salad oil
1 egg
¼ cup water
1 cup (6 ounces) semisweet chocolate morsels
½ cup chopped walnuts or pecans, optional

Preheat the oven to 350°F.

In a large bowl, with a wooden spoon, combine the cake mix, the oil, egg, and the water; beat for 1 minute.

Add the chocolate morsels and the optional nuts.

Drop the dough by heaping teaspoonfuls onto ungreased cookie sheets, and bake for 10 to 12 minutes.

Cool the cookie sheet on a wire rack for 30 seconds; then remove the cookies, and let them cool thoroughly. They may also be frozen.

Makes 3½ to 4 dozen.

COOKIE HINTS

Use shiny cookie sheets for drop and sliced cookies, as they reflect the heat away from the cookie bottoms so that they can bake evenly. Cookie sheets with a dark finish concentrate the heat on the bottoms of the cookies, causing them to burn before they are done.

Cookies turn brown because the sugar in them caramelizes at around 350°F and becomes amber, which in turn colors the cookies brown. Sugar also tenderizes the dough, causing a slight crispness to occur. Without sugar, the dough would be tough.

Never double-decker cookie sheets (or cake pans, for that matter) in your oven, as placing one cookie sheet over another interferes with the proper circulation of heat.

When making drop cookies, if you don't have enough dough to completely fill your last cookie sheet, use the bottom of a small pie or cake pan. When only one part of a cookie sheet is filled, the heat is attracted to that area, causing the cookies to brown very quickly on the bottom, and they can burn very easily.

CHOCOLATE PUFFS

Very delicate and very habit-forming.

---

1 cup (6 ounces) semisweet chocolate morsels
2 egg whites
Pinch of salt
½ cup sugar
½ teaspoon vanilla extract
½ teaspoon cider vinegar
¾ cup chopped walnuts

In the top part of a double boiler, over hot water, melt the chocolate; set it aside to cool.

Preheat the oven to 350°F.

In a medium bowl, with electric mixer at high speed, beat the egg whites and the salt until soft peaks form.

When the egg whites begin to hold their peaks, gradually add the sugar, and continue beating until stiff peaks form.

Beat the vanilla and the vinegar.

Fold in the cooled chocolate and the chopped nuts, blending with a rubber scraper until the mixture is thoroughly combined.

Drop by teaspoonfuls onto a greased cookie sheet, and bake for 8 to 10 minutes.

Cool the cookie sheet on a wire rack for 30 seconds; then remove the cookies, and let them cool thoroughly.

Makes about 2 dozen.

NEVER–TO–BE–FORGOTTEN MANDEL BREAD

One fabulous cookie!

½ cup vegetable shortening
1 cup sugar
3 eggs
3 cups flour
2 teaspoons baking powder
Pinch of salt
1 teaspoon vanilla
1 teaspoon almond extract
½ cup *each* red and green maraschino cherries, cut up
½ cup (or more) yellow raisins
1 cup (6 ounces) butterscotch morsels
½ cup chopped walnuts or almonds, optional

ICING:

½ cup sifted confectioners' sugar
1 teaspoon vanilla
1 tablespoon butter or margarine, softened
1 to 2 tablespoons warm milk

Preheat the oven to 350°F.

In a large bowl, with electric mixer at medium speed, cream the shortening and the sugar.

Add the eggs one at a time, beating well after each addition.

Sift together the flour, baking powder, and the salt; using a wooden spoon, slowly add the flour mixture to the bowl.

Stir in the vanilla and the almond extract, along with the cherries, raisins, the butterscotch morsels, and the optional nuts.

Form the dough into 3 strips, each about 12 inches long × 2 inches wide, and place all three on a large greased and floured cookie sheet.

Bake the dough for 20 to 25 minutes.

Cool the strips on a wire rack.

Meanwhile, prepare the icing: combine the sugar, vanilla, and the butter with enough warm milk to form a fairly liquid mixture.

Pour the icing over the cooled strips, and cut each strip into 12 1-inch slices.

Makes 3 dozen.

FRENCH ALMOND ROUNDS

---

1 cup flour
½ cup sugar
Pinch of salt
2 egg yolks
½ cup finely ground blanched almonds
6 tablespoons butter or margarine, softened
1 whole egg + 1 teaspoon water for glazing

Sift the flour into a medium bowl, making a well in the center.

Into the well, pour the sugar, the salt, and the egg yolks; then add the almonds and the butter.

Work the dough with your hands, pinching the sugar, salt, egg yolks, almonds, and butter into the flour.

Shape the dough into a ball; wrap it in waxed paper, and chill it for about 1 hour.

Preheat the oven to 400°F.

On a lightly floured surface, roll the dough out to ⅛-inch thickness, and with a round cookie cutter, cut it into 2-inch circles.

Brush each circle with the egg-water mixture; score the tops with a dinner fork, and place the rounds on an ungreased cookie sheet.

Bake the cookies for 10 to 12 minutes.

Let the cookie sheet cool on a wire rack for 30 seconds; then remove the rounds to the wire rack to cool thoroughly.

Makes about 2 dozen.

LEMON FINGERS

½ cup + 4 teaspoons butter or margarine, softened
½ cup sugar
1 egg
2 teaspoons grated lemon peel
1½ cups flour
1 teaspoon baking powder
1 cup raspberry or strawberry jam

ICING:

1 cup sifted confectioners' sugar
1 tablespoon water
2 teaspoons lemon juice

Preheat the oven to 400°F.

In a medium bowl, with electric mixer at medium speed, cream the butter and the sugar until it is light and fluffy.

Add the egg, and continue to beat until well combined; then beat in the grated lemon peel.

With a wooden spoon, fold the flour and baking powder into the butter mixture, working it into a dough.

Roll or shape the dough into 2 12-inch strips, and place them on a greased cookie sheet.

Using the handle of a wooden spoon, or your finger, make a groove along the center of each strip, and fill the grooves with the jam.

Bake for 10 to 15 minutes; remove the cookie sheet to a wire rack to cool.

Meanwhile, prepare the icing by combining the sugar, water, and the lemon juice in a small bowl until smooth.

Drizzle the icing over the baked strips, and when they are completely cool, cut each strip into about 15 ¾-inch slices.

Makes about 2½ dozen.

CHAPTER 5

DESSERTS

Crêpes
Mousses, Puddings, & Creams
Pies
Fruits
Sweet Treats

sugar cane

Crêpes

GÂTEAU DES CREPÊS

This crêpe dessert resembles an iced cake until it is cut and served. Then watch the surprised faces of your guests, and listen to the praise!

CRÊPES:

4 eggs
2 cups milk
2 cups flour
1 teaspoon melted butter
Additional melted butter for making crêpes

FILLING:

2 tablespoons butter or margarine
5 or 6 tart apples, peeled, cored, and coarsely chopped
1 to 2 ounces cinnamon "red hot" candy
Few drops of red food-coloring, optional
¼ cup apple brandy or apple juice
1 cup sugar
1½ cups slivered blanched almonds

TOPPING:

2 egg whites
¼ teaspoon cream of tartar
¼ cup sugar

Several hours before serving, prepare the crêpe batter: Combine the eggs, milk, flour, and 1 teaspoon of melted butter in a food processor or blender container.

Process or blend until the mixture is smooth; then let stand at room temperature for 2 hours, so that the flour dissolves completely.

To prepare the crêpes, heat a 7- or 8-inch crêpe pan over medium-high heat for about 3 minutes; brush it with some melted butter.

Using a ladle or a small measuring cup, pour about 2 tablespoons of batter into the pan, rotating the pan to insure that the batter covers the bottom (not the sides) quickly and evenly.

Cook until the crêpe is dry on top, and using a flexible spatula, turn it over; cook about 15 seconds longer, or until lightly browned.

Slide the crêpe out of the pan onto a wire rack, and repeat the process. Stack the crêpes as you cook them. Brush the pan with melted butter about every other crêpe. You should have about 20 to 22 crêpes.

To make the filling, melt the butter in a large saucepan; add the apples, the cinnamon candy, and the optional food-coloring, tossing the apples well to coat them with the butter.

Add the apple brandy or juice and the sugar; cover the saucepan with a tight-fitting lid, and cook over low heat, stirring occasionally, until the apples are soft—about 30 minutes.

Preheat the oven to 400°F.

To assemble the *gâteau*, place one crêpe on a buttered baking dish; spread about 2½ tablespoons of the apple mixture over the crêpe, and sprinkle about 1 tablespoon of the almonds on top.

Place another crêpe over the almonds, and top it with the same amount of apple mixture and almonds. Repeat the process until all the crêpes, filling, and almonds are used up, ending with a crêpe.

In a medium bowl, with electric mixer at high speed, beat the egg whites with the cream of tartar until soft peaks form.

Gradually add the sugar, a tablespoon at a time, and beat until a stiff meringue forms.

Use the meringue to ice the crêpe gateau as you would a cake.

Bake the *gâteau* for 6 to 8 minutes, or until the meringue is lightly spotted and brown.

Serve immediately by slicing into small wedges with a very sharp knife.

Serves 6 to 8.

CHOCOLATE CRÊPES

6 tablespoons flour
2 tablespoons unsweetened cocoa
Pinch of salt
2 eggs + 2 egg yolks
1 tablespoon sugar
¼ cup salad oil
⅓ cup milk
Melted butter for cooking crêpes

FILLING:

1 cup whipping cream
2 tablespoons confectioners' sugar
4 teaspoons instant coffee powder

SAUCE:

¼ cup unsweetened cocoa
½ cup sugar
½ cup light corn syrup
¼ cup table cream
1½ tablespoons butter or margarine
Pinch of salt
½ teaspoon vanilla

Several hours before serving, prepare the crêpe batter: in a food processor or blender container, combine the flour, cocoa, salt, eggs, egg yolks, sugar, salad oil, and the milk.

Process or blend until the mixture is smooth; then refrigerate the batter for 1 hour.

To prepare the crêpes, heat a 7- or 8-inch crêpe pan over medium-high heat for about 3 minutes; brush it with some melted butter.

Using a ladle or a small measuring cup, pour about 2 tablespoons of batter into the pan, rotating the pan to insure that the batter covers the bottom (not the sides) quickly and evenly.

Cook until the crêpe is dry on top, and using a flexible spatula, turn it over; cook about 15 seconds longer, or until it is nicely browned.

Slide the crêpe out of the pan onto a wire rack, and repeat the process. Stack the crêpes as you cook them. Brush the pan with melted butter about every other crêpe. You should have about 12 crêpes. Let them cool completely before proceeding with recipe.

To make the filling, place the cream in a medium bowl, and with electric mixer at high speed, whip the cream until soft peaks begin to form.

With the mixer still running, gradually add the sugar and coffee, continuing to beat until stiff peaks form. Chill the filling, while preparing the sauce.

Place the cocoa, sugar, corn syrup, cream, butter, and salt in a small, heavy saucepan, and bring to a boil, over medium heat.

Reduce the heat, and simmer the sauce for 5 minutes. Remove the pan from the heat, and stir in the vanilla.

To assemble the crêpes, place a heaping spoonful of whipped cream in the center of each crêpe, and fold the crêpe in thirds.

Place the filled crêpes, seam down, on a serving dish, and pass the chocolate sauce separately.

Serves 4 to 6.

Mousses, Puddings, & Creams

HORATIO'S CHOCOLATE CHEESE MOUSSE

I found this unique dessert in Hawaii and brought it home as a favorite.

4 packages (3 ounces each) cream cheese, softened
1½ cups sugar
1½ teaspoons vanilla
¼ cup unsweetened cocoa
1 cup whipping cream
Additional whipped cream for garnish, optional

In a large bowl, with electric mixer at medium speed, beat the cream cheese, sugar, and the vanilla until very light and fluffy—about 10 minutes. The sugar should be well dissolved; taste a little of the mixture, and if the texture is grainy, it needs to be beaten longer.

Add the cocoa, and beat until the mixture is smooth and the cocoa is dissolved.

In another large bowl, with electric mixer at high speed, whip the cream until soft peaks form.

Fold the whipped cream into the cheese mixture one half at a time, blending well with a rubber scraper.

Divide the mixture into 10 to 12 individual dessert dishes, or spoon it into a large serving bowl, and refrigerate the mousse for at least 8 hours.

If desired, garnish the dessert with additional whipped cream before serving.

Serves 10 to 12.

WHITE CHOCOLATE MOUSSE

A most distinctive recipe from chef Emil Graf of the Caribe Hilton Hotel.

---

6 ounces white chocolate (such as **Toblerone**)
⅓ cup milk
1 cup whipping cream
2 large egg whites
½ teaspoon lemon juice

Break the white chocolate into small pieces.

In a small, heavy saucepan, heat the milk over low heat, and when it is hot but not boiling, add the chocolate.

Cook, stirring, over low heat until the chocolate has melted; do not let the mixture get too hot.

Remove the saucepan from the heat, and let the milk mixture cool, stirring occasionally.

In a large bowl, with electric mixer at high speed, beat the cream until it forms stiff peaks; place it in the refrigerator.

Wash and dry the beaters, and in a medium bowl, with electric mixer at high speed, beat the egg whites just until they begin to hold soft peaks.

Add the lemon juice, and continue beating until stiff peaks form.

When the chocolate mixture has cooled, lightly fold it into the whipped cream, using a rubber scraper.

Then fold in the egg whites, being careful not to overfold.

Spoon the mousse into 6 individual dessert dishes or into a serving bowl, cover, and refrigerate until it is very cold—about 4 hours.

Serves 6.

Cream that is hard to whip will thicken quickly when you add a few drops of lemon juice to the bowl.

Never beat egg whites in a plastic bowl, as you will not get good volume.

To preserve egg yolks, place them in a small bowl, and cover with 2 tablespoons of salad oil. Store in the refrigerator, and they will stay soft and fresh for a few days. Egg yolks can be used in puddings, custards, to make homemade mayonnaise or hollandaise sauce, or, as a last resort, can be added to egg mixtures for extra richness.

RICE PUDDING

The old-fashioned, creamy kind.

½ cup raisins
½ cup boiling water
⅓ cup long grain raw white rice
1½ cups water
1⅓ cups whole or evaporated milk
⅓ cup sugar
1 teaspoon cornstarch
¼ teaspoon salt
½ teaspoon vanilla
1 tablespoon butter or margarine
2 egg yolks

Place the raisins in a small bowl, and pour the boiling water on top; set aside while preparing the rest of the recipe.

Place the rice and the water in a medium saucepan, and bring it to a boil.

Stir the rice; cover the saucepan, reduce the heat, and simmer the rice until it is very tender and most of the liquid has been absorbed—about 25 minutes.

Add the milk, sugar, cornstarch, and salt, and bring to a boil again; boil for 1 minute, stirring.

Remove the saucepan from the heat, and stir in the vanilla and the butter.

In a small bowl, lightly beat the egg yolks. Stir a little of the rice mixture into the egg yolks; then return the egg yolk mixture to the saucepan.

Place the saucepan over low heat, and very gently cook it, being careful not to let the egg yolks curdle. Remove the saucepan from the heat before the pudding reaches the boiling point.

Drain the water from the raisins, and add them to the pudding.

Serve the pudding at room temperature or well chilled.

Serves 4.

HORATIO'S BURNT CRÈME

Another name for this rich dessert is crème brûlée.

---

1 pint whipping cream
4 egg yolks
½ cup sugar
1 tablespoon vanilla
Additional sugar for topping

Preheat the oven to 350°F.

In a small saucepan over low heat, heat the cream until bubbles form around the edges of the pan. Remove from the heat, and let the cream cool until it is tepid.

In a large bowl, with electric mixer at medium speed, beat the egg yolks and the sugar together until they are thick and lemony—about 5 to 7 minutes.

Gradually beat in the cooled cream, beating until smooth.

Stir in the vanilla, and pour the mixture into 6 6-ounce custard cups.

Place the cups in a shallow baking dish, and pour in about 1 inch of hot water.

Bake the crème for 45 minutes, or until a knife inserted in the center comes out clean.

Remove the cups from the water, and refrigerate them until well chilled.

Preheat the oven to Broil.

Sprinkle about 2 teaspoons of sugar over each cup, and carefully place the cups on the top rack of the oven.

Quickly broil the crème just long enough to turn the sugar a rich brown; be careful not to burn the desserts.

Return the cups to the refrigerator, and chill them until serving.

Serves 6.

RUM FLAN

6 tablespoons sugar
1 cup half-and-half
2 egg yolks
1 whole egg
1 teaspoon dark rum
1 teaspoon grated orange peel

Preheat the oven to 325°F.

Heat 4 tablespoons of the sugar in a small, heavy saucepan over medium heat, stirring constantly, until the sugar begins to melt and turns light golden brown (caramelizes).

Immediately remove the saucepan from the heat, and pour the caramelized sugar into 4 5-ounce custard cups; let the sugar cool.

In a medium bowl, with a wire whisk, beat the half-and-half, egg yolks, whole egg, the rum, orange peel, and the remaining sugar; continue beating until the mixture is smooth, and pour it over the cooled caramel.

Place the cups in a shallow baking dish, and pour in about 1 inch of hot water.

Bake the flan for 1 hour, or until a knife inserted in the center comes out clean.

Let the cups cool, and then refrigerate them until the flan is well chilled.

Serves 4.

FLAN RAPHAEL

A classic, and one of the best flans I have ever had anywhere.

1½ cups sugar
1 tablespoon water
1 can (14 ounces) Eagle brand sweetened condensed milk
2 milk cans of water
4 eggs
1 teaspoon vanilla

Preheat the oven to 350°F.

In a large skillet, over medium heat, carefully brown the sugar and the tablespoon of water, stirring constantly; do not let it burn or turn black.

When the sugar has completely melted and has a dark brown caramel color, remove it from the heat.

Pour the caramel into 8 to 10 individual custard cups or into a large ring mold.

In a medium bowl, combine the remaining ingredients, mixing well.

Pour the mixture evenly over the caramel in the custard cups or the mold.

Fill a baking pan large enough to hold the cups of the mold with 1 inch of boiling water.

Place the custard cups or mold into the pan, and bake for about 1 hour, or until a knife inserted in the center comes out clean.

Serve the flan well chilled.

Serves 8 to 10.

TOASTED ALMOND

A creamy drink that can be served in lieu of dessert; even non-drinkers will enjoy it.

½ cup Amaretto (or other almond liqueur)
½ cup crème de cacao (or other chocolate liqueur)
1 cup half-and-half
Ice cubes

Place the Amaretto, the crème de cacao and the half-and-half in a blender container.

Fill the container with enough ice cubes to reach above the top of the liquid (so that the drink will reach a frozen stage).

Blend at high speed until the ice cubes are well crushed, and pour into goblets or large wine glasses.

Serves 4.

Pies

CHEESE PIE

4 eggs, separated
¾ cup sugar
1 tablespoon lemon juice
1 teaspoon grated lemon peel
1 teaspoon grated orange peel
1 small container (15 ounces) ricotta cheese
1 teaspoon vanilla
½ cup yellow raisins
½ cup whipping cream
1 tablespoon kirsch (white cherry liqueur)

In a large bowl, with electric mixer at medium speed, beat the egg yolks and sugar until thick and lemony—about 15 minutes.

Preheat the oven to 350°F.

Add the lemon juice and the lemon and orange peel to the egg yolk mixture, beating well.

With the electric mixer at low speed, add the cheese and the vanilla.

Wash and dry the beaters thoroughly, and in another large bowl, with electric mixer at high speed, beat the egg whites until stiff peaks form.

Fold the beaten egg whites into the cheese mixture so that no clumps of egg whites remain; then fold in the raisins.

Place the mixture in a buttered 9-inch pie pan, and bake for 30 minutes, or until a knife inserted in the center comes out clean.

Cool the pie on a wire rack.

In a medium bowl, with electric mixer at high speed, beat the cream with the kirsch, and spread the mixture evenly over the pie. Chill the pie.

Serves 6 to 8.

KEY LIME PIE I

This dessert, which somewhat resembles lemon meringue pie, originated in the Florida Keys.

---

3 egg yolks
½ cup freshly squeezed lime juice
1 teaspoon grated lime peel
1 can (14 ounces) sweetened condensed milk
2 to 3 drops green food-coloring
1 baked 9-inch pie shell
4 egg whites
½ cup sugar

Preheat the oven to 350°F.

In a medium bowl, with electric mixer at medium speed or with a wire whisk, beat the egg yolks until they are thick and lemony.

Add all of the lime juice except for 1 teaspoon, which you should reserve for the meringue topping; also add the lime peel.

Beat in the condensed milk and enough food coloring to attain a pleasant green tint.

Pour the mixture into the baked pie shell.

In a large bowl, with electric mixer at high speed, beat the egg whites until soft peaks form.

Gradually beat in the sugar and the reserved lime juice, beating until the meringue is stiff and glossy.

Spread the meringue over the pie filling, bringing it to the crust, and swirling it with a spatula.

Bake the pie for 15 minutes, or until the meringue is light brown. Cool the pie on a wire rack, and then chill it well before serving.

Serves 6 to 8.

KEY LIME PIE II

¼ cup freshly squeezed lime juice
½ teaspoon salt
1 can (8½ ounces) crushed pineapple, undrained
1 can (14 ounces) sweetened condensed milk
2 to 3 drops green food-coloring
1 9-inch baked pie shell
1 cup whipping cream
2 tablespoons confectioners' sugar
1 square (1 ounce) unsweetened chocolate

Several hours before serving, combine the lime juice, salt, pineapple and its juice, and the condensed milk in a medium bowl, mixing well.

Add enough food coloring to attain a pleasant green tint, and pour the mixture into the baked pie shell. Refrigerate for several hours.

Just before serving, in a large bowl, with electric mixer at high speed, beat the cream and the sugar until stiff peaks form.

Spread the whipped cream over the pie filling.

Grate the chocolate over the whipped cream. (If not serving the pie right away, return it to the refrigerator.)

Serves 6 to 8.

NO–BAKE STRAWBERRY PIE

¾ cup sugar
3 tablespoons cornstarch
1½ cups warm water
1 package (3 ounces) strawberry gelatin
1 quart fresh strawberries
1 9-inch baked pie shell
1 cup whipping cream

Place the sugar in a small, heavy saucepan, and stir in the cornstarch.

Gradually add the water, stirring well; cook the mixture over medium heat, stirring constantly, until it is smooth and thickened.

Remove the saucepan from the heat, and stir in the gelatin. Set aside to cool.

Meanwhile, wash, hull, and slice the strawberries. (If you like, you can set aside a few berries for garnish.)

Gently fold the sliced berries into the gelatin mixture, and pour it into the baked pie shell; refrigerate for several hours.

In a large bowl, with electric mixer at high speed, whip the cream until stiff peaks form, and spread the whipped cream over the pie. If desired, garnish with some reserved berries. Return the pie to the refrigerator if not serving right away.

Serves 6 to 8.

HINT

Never wash strawberries or remove the hulls until just before using them. Washing removes the natural protective outer layer, and the hulls protect the berry, helping to preserve its flavor, texture, and nutrients.

WATERMELON CHIFFON PIE

A refreshingly light—and different—summertime dessert.

1½ cups mashed ripe watermelon
3 eggs, separated
Pinch of salt
2 tablespoons lemon juice
1 envelope unflavored gelatin
½ cup sugar
½ cup whipping cream
1 8- or 9-inch baked pie shell

The day before serving, mix the mashed watermelon with the 3 egg yolks, the salt, lemon juice, and gelatin in the top part of a double boiler. Let the mixture stand for 5 minutes.

Place the top part of the double boiler over boiling water, and cook the watermelon mixture, stirring constantly, until it is translucent and coats a wooden spoon—about 15 minutes.

Remove the mixture from the heat, and let it cool; then chill the mixture until it has a syrupy consistency.

In a medium bowl, with electric mixer at high speed, beat the egg whites until soft peaks form.

Gradually add the sugar, and continue beating until the meringue is stiff and glossy.

In another bowl, with electric mixer at high speed, whip the cream until stiff peaks form.

Fold the meringue into the watermelon mixture, blending well; then fold in the whipped cream, mixing well.

Pour the mixture into the baked pie shell, and refrigerate it overnight.

If desired, you can garnish the pie with watermelon balls.

Serves 6 to 8.

Pie crusts will be easier to make if all ingredients are cool.

Most pie crust recipes call for 1 cup of flour and $\frac{1}{3}$ cup of shortening. If you increase the shortening to $\frac{1}{2}$ cup, you will have a flakier pie crust.

Use glass pie pans, as they hold the heat longer so that the crust will continue to brown after the pie pan has been removed from the oven.

Fruits

BANANAS FOSTER MEXICAN

¼ cup butter or margarine
4 large firm bananas, sliced in half lengthwise
1 cup dark brown sugar
Juice of 2 oranges
Grated peel of 1 orange
½ cup sour cream
½ cup sifted confectioners' sugar

In a large skillet, slowly melt the butter, being careful not to let it turn brown.

Add the banana halves, and gently cook them for 1 minute on each side.

Combine the sugar, the orange juice, and the peel, and pour this mixture over the bananas.

Simmer the bananas in the sauce over low heat for 15 minutes, or until the bananas are tender. Turn the bananas once, and spoon some of the sauce over them as they cook.

Serve the bananas warm with a mixture of the sour cream and confectioners' sugar spooned on top.

Serves 4.

Note: The bananas can also be served with scoops of ice cream instead of the sour cream. Or flambé them by gently heating ¼ cup of rum and then carefully igniting the rum as you pour it over the bananas and the sauce. Serve the bananas as soon as the flames are extinguished.

BANANAS FLAMBÉ

Here is a French version of a dessert that originated on the French Caribbean island of Martinique, where it was customarily flambéed with rum.

---

8 firm bananas, sliced in half lengthwise
2 teaspoons grated lemon peel
Juice of 1 lemon
½ to ⅔ cup sugar
¼ cup unsalted butter
¼ cup curaçao
⅓ cup cognac

Preheat the oven to 400°F.

Place the banana halves in a single layer in a large, shallow, buttered baking dish.

Sprinkle the lemon peel over the bananas, and then the lemon juice and the sugar.

Break the butter up into small pieces, and distribute it evenly over the bananas.

Bake the bananas, uncovered, for 10 to 15 minutes, or until the fruit is soft and appears glazed. While they are baking, baste the bananas with the melting sugar and butter that accumulates in the baking dish.

Remove the baking dish from the oven, and pour the curaçao over the bananas.

In a small pan or butter-melter, gently heat the cognac; start to pour it over the bananas, and as you do so, carefully ignite it with a long wooden match. (You can do this at the table for dramatic effect.) Serve at once.

Serves 8.

Note: If you wish, orange peel and orange juice can be substituted for the lemon, and the curaçao can be eliminated. You can also flambé the bananas with rum instead of cognac.

HEAVENLY GRAPES

The name says it all.

---

4 cups seedless green grapes
2 cups sour cream
3 tablespoons dark brown sugar
1½ tablespoons white crème de cacao

In a large bowl, combine all the ingredients, mixing well.

Chill the mixture for several hours, to allow the flavors to develop.

To serve, spoon the grapes and their sauce into 6 to 8 champagne or wine glasses.

Serves 6 to 8.

Note: Fresh peaches, peeled and sliced, may be substituted for the grapes.

BRANDIED FRUITS

---

2 cups fresh orange sections, with white membrane
   removed
2 cups canned pineapple chunks, drained (fresh
   pineapple can be used)
2 cups peeled and sliced pears (or 2 cups pear halves,
   drained and sliced)
2 cups peeled and sliced peaches (or 2 cups canned
   sliced peaches, drained)
2 cups seedless green grapes, cut in half
2½ cups sugar
2½ cups dark brown sugar
1 6-inch stick of cinnamon, broken in half
1 pint apricot brandy

One week before serving, combine all the fruits in a large
bowl.

Add both the sugars, and let the mixture stand for 3 hours,
stirring once or twice.

Add the cinnamon stick and the brandy.

Loosely cover the bowl, and let the mixture stand at room
temperature for 1 week, stirring once a day.

Serve with toothpicks or bamboo skewers.

Serves 12.

HINT

To enhance the flavor and freshness of pears, prunes,
apricots, nectarines, and peaches, wash the fruit in warm
water, and dry it on a cookie sheet in a 100°F oven for
20 to 25 minutes. Store the fruit in tightly covered jars
or plastic bags in the refrigerator.

PEARS EXOTIC

2 cans (16 ounces each) pear halves, well drained
2 tablespoons unsweetened cocoa
1 egg
2 cups sifted confectioners' sugar
2 tablespoons melted butter or margarine
½ cup whipping cream
1 tablespoon rum

For 6 servings, you will need 12 pear halves.

Several hours before serving, place 1 teaspoon of cocoa in the center of 6 pear halves, and cover with the other 6 halves. Chill the pears for 6 hours.

Meanwhile, prepare the sauce: In a medium bowl, with electric mixer at medium speed, beat the egg with the confectioners' sugar and the melted butter until smooth.

In another medium bowl, with electric mixer at high speed, whip the cream until stiff peaks form.

Fold the whipped cream and the rum into the egg mixture, and chill the sauce.

To serve, place one whole pear in each of 6 serving dishes, and pour the sauce evenly over each one.

Serves 6.

PEARS ALI BABA

The perfect finale to an elaborate dinner.

---

6 to 8 firm fresh pears
3 cups dry white wine
½ cup sugar
2-inch piece of vanilla bean
2 cups fresh strawberries
2 cups fresh raspberries (or 1 12-ounce box of frozen
    raspberries, thawed and drained)
3 cups whipping cream
½ cup sifted confectioners' sugar
⅓ cup red port wine (approximately)

Several hours or the day before serving, carefully peel the pears, keeping the surface as smooth as possible, and leaving the stems on.

In a large skillet, gently heat the wine, and dissolve the sugar in it.

Lay the pears in the sweetened wine, add the vanilla bean, and bring the wine to a boil.

Reduce the heat, and poach the fruit until it is tender but still firm—about 15 to 20 minutes.

Remove the skillet from the heat, and allow the pears to cool in the wine mixture. Then chill the pears in the poaching liquid until icy cold.

Meanwhile, wash and hull the strawberries, and press them through a sieve with a wooden spoon; crush the raspberries, and force them through a sieve to remove all the seeds.

Mix the 2 fruit purees together, and chill them. The mixture should be very cold, and thick enough to mask the pears.

In a large bowl, with electric mixer at high speed, whip 2 cups of the cream until soft peaks form; add the confectioners' sugar, and continue beating until the cream is very firm.

Fold in the port wine, using only as much as the cream will hold without becoming too soft or liquid. Chill the mixture.

In another bowl, with electric mixer at high speed, whip the remaining cup of cream until stiff peaks form, and chill it. (This cream is to be used for decoration.)

To assemble the dessert, cover the bottom of a round, shallow serving dish with the port-flavored whipped cream.

Arrange the pears carefully on top, and spoon the first puree carefully over each pear, masking the entire surface.

Spoon any remaining puree around the base of the pears to cover the whipped cream.

Decorate the base of the pears with the plain whipped cream, using a pastry bag with a star tip.

Serves 6 to 8.

FRUIT SURPRISE

No one can identify the fruit used in this exotic dessert.

6 firm apples suitable for cooking, peeled
1 jar (8 ounces) of honey
8 squares (1 ounce each) semisweet chocolate

Slice the apples so that they resemble orange sections.

Place the honey in a heavy saucepan, and heat it over very low heat.

Add the apple slices, and cook, stirring constantly, until they are translucent.

Remove the apples from the pan, and cool the slices on waxed paper.

In the top part of a double boiler over hot water, carefully melt the chocolate.

Dip the cooled apple sections in the warm chocolate; or place the apple sections on a rack over a shallow pan, and pour the melted chocolate over them.

Let the slices stand at room temperature to allow the chocolate to become firm; then chill the chocolate-covered slices well before serving.

To serve, spear the slices with toothpicks or bamboo skewers.

Serves 6.

CRANBERRY FLUMMERY

A new way to use cranberries, this came from a friend in Ohio.

---

2 cups fresh cranberries, washed and dried
1⅓ cups sugar
½ cup chopped walnuts
¾ cup butter or margarine, softened
2 eggs
1 cup flour
1 teaspoon almond extract

Preheat the oven to 325°F; grease a 10-inch pie pan or a small, shallow baking dish.

Spread the cranberries evenly over the bottom of the prepared pan, and sprinkle them with ⅓ cup of the sugar and the walnuts.

In a large bowl, with electric mixer at medium speed, cream the butter with the remaining sugar until light and fluffy.

Add the eggs one at a time, beating well after each addition.

With the electric mixer at low speed, add the flour and the almond extract; pour the batter over the cranberries.

Bake for 35 to 40 minutes, or until the topping is golden brown.

Cool the pan on a wire rack, and serve at room temperature with vanilla ice cream or whipped cream, if desired.

Serves 6 to 8.

Sweet Treats

APRICOT BALLS

This makes a nice gift from your kitchen—if your family members don't devour it first!

---

1 orange, peeled and divided into sections
1 pound dried apricots
Juice of 1 lemon
Juice of 1 orange
2 cups sugar
2½ cups finely ground pecans
¾ cup sifted confectioners' sugar

Remove any membrane from the orange sections.

Place the orange sections and the apricots in a food processor fitted with a steel blade, and process until the fruits are chopped into very fine pieces.

Add the lemon and orange juice and the sugar, mixing well.

Place the mixture in a saucepan and cook over low heat, stirring constantly, for 8 to 10 minutes.

Remove the mixture from the heat, and let cool.

Add the pecans, and shape the mixture into 1-inch balls.

Roll the balls in the confectioners' sugar, and store them in an airtight container. They will keep this way for several weeks.

Makes about 6 dozen.

BOURBON BALLS

These are nice to serve—and give—around holiday time.

---

1 box (10 ounces) vanilla wafers
2 tablespoons unsweetened cocoa
1½ cups sifted confectioners' sugar
1 cup finely chopped walnuts
3 tablespoons light corn syrup
¼ to ⅓ cup bourbon

Break the vanilla wafers into large pieces, and using a food
processor or a blender, pulverize the cookies into fine crumbs.

Transfer the crumbs to a large bowl, and add the cocoa, 1
cup of the confectioners' sugar, and the nuts.

Add the syrup and the bourbon, mixing well. (If the mixture
seems too dry, you can add more bourbon, but don't overdo
it.)

Form the mixture into 1-inch balls; they may feel crumbly
at first, but as you squeeze them, they will become more moist.

Roll the balls in the remaining confectioners' sugar, and
store them in a tightly covered container for a few days to
"ripen." The bourbon balls will keep for several weeks.

Makes about 3 dozen.

HOLIDAY NUTS

2 egg whites
1 cup sugar
½ teaspoon salt
1 pound pecan halves
½ cup butter or margarine

Preheat the oven to 300°F.

In a medium bowl, with electric mixer at high speed, beat the egg whites until soft peaks begin to form.

Slowly add the sugar and the salt, beating until the mixture forms a stiff meringue.

Fold in the pecan halves.

Place the butter in a 15 × 11-inch jelly-roll pan, and melt it in the oven.

Spread the nut mixture over the melted butter, and return the pan to the oven to bake for 45 minutes; stir every 15 minutes.

Turn the nut mixture out onto paper towels to dry and cool thoroughly.

Break the mixture up into large pieces, and store them in an airtight container.

Save any scraps for use as a topping on ice cream or fruit salad.

Makes about 2½ dozen.

CHINESE NO–BAKE "COOKIES"

Easy and unusual; watch them go!

---

1 cup (6 ounces) semisweet chocolate morsels
1 cup (6 ounces) butterscotch morsels
1 can (10½ ounces) chow mein noodles
1 cup chopped walnuts, almonds, or pecans

In the top part of a double boiler, over hot water, melt the chocolate and the butterscotch morsels.

Remove the mixture from the heat, and stir in the chow mein noodles and the nuts, mixing thoroughly.

Drop by tablespoonfuls onto a cookie sheet that has been covered with waxed paper, and refrigerate the cookies until they are firm.

With a metal spatula, remove the cookies from the waxed paper, and store them in a container in the refrigerator.

Makes about 2 dozen.

Converting to the Metric System

The figures in the little tables in the text have been rounded off to the nearest whole number or convenient fraction. A more accurate figure may be printed in these tables, but you can work out an even more accurate figure by making the conversion yourself.

Temperature   F. = Fahrenheit   C. = Celsius (Centigrade)

Conversion factor, Fahrenheit to Celsius: Subtract 32 from the Fahrenheit figure; multiply the result by 5, then divide that figure by 9.

Conversion factor, Celsius to Fahrenheit: Multiply Celsius figure by 9, divide by 5, and add 32.

° FAHRENHEIT	° CELSIUS	
32	0	(water freezes)
110	43.3	
115	46.1	
170	76.7	
212	100	(water boils)
325	163	
350	177	
370	187.7	
375	190.5	
400	204.4	
425	218.3	
450	232	
500	260	

OUNCES AND POUNDS

Conversion factor, ounces to grams: Multiply ounce figure by 28.3 to get number of grams. 1 gram $\times$ 1000 = 1 kilogram. Conversion factor, grams to ounces: Multiply gram figure by .0353 to get number of ounces.

OUNCES	GRAMS
¼	7
1	28.3
3	84.8
4	113.2
6	169.8
8 (½ pound)	226.4
10	283
¼ pound	113.2
½ pound	226.4
1 pound	453.6 = 0.4536 kilogram

Conversion factor, pounds into grams: Multiply pound figure by 453.59 to get number of grams.

INCHES

Conversion factor, inches to centimeters: Multiply inch figure by 2.54 to get number of centimeters.

Conversion factor, centimeters to inches: Multiply centimeter figure by .39 to get number of inches.

INCHES	CENTIMETERS
$\frac{1}{16}$	.159
$\frac{1}{8}$	.318
$\frac{1}{4}$	.636
$\frac{1}{2}$	1.27
1	2.54
$1\frac{1}{2}$	3.81
2	5.08
10	25.4
15	38.1

1 centimeter = 10 millimeters.
1 meter = 100 centimeters = 1000 millimeters.

LIQUID VOLUME MEASURES

Liquids include water, milk, wine, and also such apparent solids as butter and sugar, both of which count as liquids in baking. The volume measures will be filled exactly, to the brim for spoon measures, to the marked levels for cups. The teaspoon measure equals ⅓ tablespoon; the tablespoon measure equals ½ ounce; the cup measure equals 8 ounces; the quart measure equals 2 pounds. For quick conversion, 1 liter can be substituted for 1 quart.

TEASPOONS	GRAMS
¼	1.17
½	2.34
1	4.7
2	9.4
3 (1 tablespoon)	14.3

TABLESPOONS	GRAMS
1	14.3
2 (1 ounce)	28.3
3	42.4
4 (¼ cup)	56.7
6	84.8
8 (½ cup)	114

CUPS	LITERS
¼	.059
⅓	.079
½	.118 (118.2 cubic centimeters)
⅔	.158
¾	.177
1	.236
1½	.354
2	.473
4 (1 quart)	.946
5	1.18
8 (2 quarts)	1.89
10 quarts	9.46

Index

Asparagus, Fried Beer Batter, 162
Avocado
  Boats, Salmon, 125
  Guacamole, 39
  Quiche, Artichoke Heart and,
    126
  Salad, Orange, 169
  Soup, Velvet, 40

B

Bacon, Watermelon Wrap-Ups, 14
Baklava, 221–22
Bambe Sauce, 50
Banana(s)
  Beef Filets with, 50
  Cake, Walnut, 211
  Flambées, 253
  Foster Mexican, 253
  Salad, Heavenly, 166
  Storing, 254
Barbecue Sauce, 52–53
Beef, 47–69
  with Bananas and Bambe Sauce,
    Filets, 50
  Barbecue, Stokes, 52–53
  Brisket, Best Ever, 57
  Cannelloni, 67–69
  Chicken Fried Steak, 58
  Colorado Casserole, 64–65
  and Eggplant Provençale, 54–56
  Empanadas, 62–63
  Lasagne, Zucchini, 66
  Meatballs, 64
    Reuben, with Corned, 15
    in Sour Cream and Dill
      Sauce, 60–61
  with Mustard (Boeuf
    Moutarde), 51–52
  Wellington, 47–49
  Zucchini Lasagne, 66
  Zucchini Stuffed with, 65
Beer Batter Asparagus, Fried, 162
Blanquette de Veau, 75–76
Boeuf Moutarde, 51–52
Bombe, Three Cheese, 23

Bourbon
  Balls, 262
  Brownies, Double-Frosted,
    219–20
Brandied Fruits, 255
Bread, 179–86
  Apricot-Walnut, 187
  Calzone, 181–82
  Casale Italian, 179–80
  Corn, Jalapeño, 188
  Croissants, 183–84
  Crumbs, Substituting for, 3
  Ice Cream Muffins, 189
  Jalapeño Corn, 188
  Oatmeal-Molasses, 185
  Oatmeal Quick, 186
  Quick, 186–89
  Yeast, 179–85
Broccoli with Lemon, 164
Brownies, Bourbon, 219–20
Burnt Crème, Horatio's, 242
Butter
  Adding Oil to, 73
  to Baste Poultry, 103
  vs. Margarine, 71
  Substituting for, 3
  Substituting Whipped, 193
Buttermilk, Substituting for, 3

C

Cabbage
  Fruited Cole Slaw, 167
  to Prevent Odor, 167
  Waldorf Salad, 168
Cakes, 190–213
  Apple, Jewish, 209
  Apple-Walnut, 208
  Banana-Walnut, 211
  Carrot-Macadamia Nut, 210
  Cheesecake, Chocolate, 192–93
  Cheesecake, New York–Style,
    190–91
  Chocolate
    Cheesecake, 192–93
    Cream Slices, 199–200

Dips
  Artichoke, 35
  Chilies Rellenos, 36
  Guacamole, 39
  Mushroom, 27
  to Serve, 35
Dolmathes, 31–32
Drink, Toasted Almond, 245
Dumplings, Spinach (Gnocchi
    Verdi), 163–64
Duxelles, Veal, 72–73

E

Éclairs, 223
Eggplant
  and Beef Provençale, 54–56
  Mélange, 155
  Ratatouille Niçoise, 156
  Soup, 44
Egg Rolls, 19–20
Eggs
  Artichokes Stuffed with, 34
  to Boil, 34
  Omelette Piperade, 132–33
  Omelettes, Hint for, 133
  to Store and Use Yolks, 240
  Substituting for Yolks, 4
  Temperature for Using, 196
  Whipping Whites, 240
Empanadas, 62–63

F

First Course. See Appetizers and
    First Courses
Fish (and Seafood), 110–25. See
    also specific kinds
  Broiling, Hints for, 113
  Buying, 114
  Sauces, Hints for, 111
  Simply Delicious, 111
  "What Is This Made Of?," 112
Five Chinese Spices, 18
Flan, 243–44

Raphael, 244
Rum, 243
Flounder
  à l'Italienne, 113
  Simply Delicious, 111
  "What Is This Made Of?," 112
Flour
  Substituting for, 4
  as Thickener, 77
Flummery, Cranberry, 260
Fritters, Corn, 150
Fruit, 252–60. See also specific
    kinds
  Brandied, 255
  Buying Fresh, 9–10
  Cole Slaw with, 167
  Compote, Jack-o'-Lantern, 159
  Keeping, 255
    Dried, 262
  to Prevent from Turning
      Brown, 24
  Salad, Heavenly, 166
  Soup, Ambrosia, 43
  Surprise, 259
Fudge, Texas (Cheese), 22

G

Garlic, Substituting for, 4
Gâteau des Crêpes, 233–35
Gazpacho Salad, 171
Ginger, Substituting for, 4
Glazes (for Fresh Ham), 80–81
  Apple, 81
  Apricot, 80
  Chinese, 81
  Grape, 80
  Orange Honey, 80
  Pineapple, 80
Gnocchi Verdi, 163–64
Grape(s)
  Glaze, 80
  Heavenly, 254
  Leaves, for Dolmathes, 31–32
Gravy
  Butter in, 71
  Cream, 59
Guacamole, 39

H

Haddock, Simply Delicious, 111
Halibut, "What Is This Made
  Of?," 112
Ham. *See also* Prosciutto
  Quiche Lorraine with, 82–83
  Fresh, Roast, 79–81
  Torta Primavera with, 84–85
Herbs and Spices, 7–8
  Substituting for, 4
Herring Salad, 174
Honey, Substituting for, 4–5

I

Ice Cream Muffins, 189
Inches, Converting, 267

K

Kabobs, Shrimp, 116
Kooftah Curry, 90
Kugel, Noodle, 144–45

L

Lamb, 88–90
  Kooftah Curry, 90
  Ragout, 88–89
Lasagne
  Chicken, 108–9
  Seafood Style, 115–16
  Zucchini, 66
Laurel Rice, 139
Lemon
  Angel Cake, 212–13
  Fingers, 230
  Juice, Substituting for, 5
  Rice, 142
  Roasted Capon, 91–92

Lime Pie, Key, 247–48
Liver, Chicken
  Cannelloni with, 67–69
  Chicken Lasagne with, 108
  Pâté, for Beef Wellington,
    47–48
  Pâté, Tabibian, 13–14

M

Macadamia Nut-Carrot Cake, 210
Mandel Bread, 228–29
Mango Sauce, Bambe, 50
Margarine
  vs. Butter, 71
  Substituting Whipped, 193
Measures, 265–68
  Dry vs. Liquid, 103
  Liquid Volume, Converting, 268
Meat. *See also* specific meats
  Appetizers, 13–15
Meatballs
  Colorado Casserole, 64–65
  Kooftah Curry, 90
  in Sour Cream and Dill Sauce,
    60–61
Metric System, 265–68
Milk, Substituting for, 5
Molasses Bread, Oatmeal-, 185
Mousse, 238–39
  Cake, Chocolate, 194–96
  Chocolate Cheese, 239
  White Chocolate, 239
Muffins, Ice Cream, 189
Mushroom(s)
  Dip, 27
  Noodle Casserole, 143
  Puffs, 30
  Roll-Ups, 29
  Soup, Cream of, 42
  Spinach Roulade Filling, 128–29
  Stuffed with Clams, 28
  Substituting for, 5
  Veal Duxelles, 72–73
Mustard, Substituting for, 5

Q

Quatre Épices, 165
Quesadillas Fang, 126
Quiche
    Avocado and Artichoke Heart,
      126
    Lorraine, 82–83

R

Raisins
    to Store, 159
    Substituting for, 5
Raspberries, Pears Ali Baba with,
    257–58
Ratatouille, Niçoise, 156
Red Snapper, Baked, 114
Rice, 139–42
    African Chicken with, 102
    Confetti, 141
    Dolmathes, 31–32
    Hints on, 140
    Laurel, 139
    Lemon, 142
    Pudding, 241
    Salad, 172
    Salad, Magic, 173
Roulade, Spinach, 128–29
Rum Flan, 243

S

Salads, 166–74
    Cabbage Waldorf, 168
    Fruited Cole Slaw, 167
    Gazpacho, 171
    Heavenly, 166
    Herb Blend for, 8
    Herring, 174
    Orange Avocado, 169
    Pepperoni, 170
    Rice, 172
    Rice, Magic, 173

Salami
    Smooth as Silk with, 26
    Torta Primavera with, 84–85
Salmon
    Avocado Boats, 125
    Pâté, 18
Salsa Pederson, 130
Sauces. *See also* Glazes
    Bambe (Mango), 50
    Barbecue, 52–53
    Cheese, Mornay, 128–29
    Chinese Glazing, 81
    Curry, 70–71
    for Fish, Hints on, 111
    Mango, Bambe, 50
    Marinara, Meatless, 134–35
    Mornay, 128–29
    Salsa Pederson, 130
    Sour Cream, 165
    Sour Cream and Dill, 60–61
    Thickening, 77
    Tomato, Marinara, 134–35
    Velouté, 105–6
Sausage. *See also* Pepperoni;
      Salami
    Chicken Breasts Stuffed with, 95
    Tostadas Fans with, 86–87
Scallops
    Coquilles St. Jacques Monte
      Cristo, 124–25
    with Fragrant Sauce, 16–17
Scampi Bread, 120–21
Seafood. *See* Fish (and Seafood)
Shallots, Selecting, 92
Shrimp, 115–22
    Curry, 118–19
    Egg Rolls, 19–20
    Kabobs, 116
    Kiev, 117–18
    Lasagne, Seafood Style, 115–16
    Monterey Bay, 121–22
    Pâté, 17
    Scampi Bread, 120–21
Snapper, Baked, 114
Sole
    Simply Delicious, 111
    Veronique, 110–11
    "What Is This Made Of?," 112

Watermelon
  Chiffon Pie, 250
  Wrap-Ups, 14
Wine, Substituting for, 6
Worcestershire Sauce, Substituting
    for, 6

Y

Yogurt, Substituting for, 6

Z

Ziti Casserole, 134–35
Zucchini
  Lasagne, 66
  Ratatouille Niçoise, 156
  Stuffed, 65
  Tangy, 157